Advance Praise for

Leading with a Critical Spirit

"In these times of overwhelming uncertainty, Leading with a Critical Spirit urges educational leaders to move away from technical managerial approaches to leadership and begin to bring their whole selves into the work of leading the field. Now we see mind, body, and spirit as essential elements of educational innovation, reform, and leadership."
—Gloria Ladson-Billings Emerita, FBA Immediate Past President, National Academy of Education Fellow, The British Academy Fellow, American Academy of Arts and Sciences Fellow, American Educational Research Association

"Michael Dantley lovingly and firmly calls on scholars and practitioners in educational leadership to dig deeper in personal agency to redefine their work for greater impact. To support that "calling", he guides them toward a deeper examination of critical spirituality and its power to transform educational leaders."
—Mark Anthony Gooden Christian A. Johnson Endeavor Professor in Educational Leadership, Director, Endeavor Antiracist & Restorative Leadership Initiative, Chair, Department of Organization and Leadership, Teachers College, Columbia University

"As we continue to live through this Dark Night of the Soul in so many areas of our lives, it is a true gift to have a text like this to enter our space to speak life to us in the field of educational leadership and beyond. Dr. Dantley gas gifted us a blessing, a balm in Gilead through his words and ideas in these six chapters. After all six is the number of soul integration."
—Judy A. Alston Chair and Professor, Department of Educational Leadership, Miami University

Leading with a Critical Spirit

Education and Struggle

Peter McLaren and Michael A. Peters
Series Editors

Vol. 25

Michael E. Dantley

Leading with a Critical Spirit

New Strategies for Educational Leaders

PETER LANG
Lausanne • Berlin • Bruxelles • Chennai • New York • Oxford

Library of Congress Cataloging-in-Publication Data

Names: Dantley, Michael E., author.
Title: Leading with a critical spirit: new strategies for educational leaders / Michael E. Dantley.
Description: First edition. | New York: Peter Lang, [2023] | Series: Education and struggle, 2168-6432; volume 25 | Includes bibliographical references and index.
Identifiers: LCCN 2023033528 (print) | LCCN 2023033529 (ebook) | ISBN 9781636674025 (paperback: alk. paper) | ISBN 9781636674063 (pdf)
Subjects: LCSH: Educational leadership.
Classification: LCC LB2806. D238 2023 (print) | LCC LB2806 (ebook) | DDC 371.2/011–dc23/eng/20230824
LC record available at https://lccn.loc.gov/2023033528
LC ebook record available at https://lccn.loc.gov/2023033529
DOI - 10.3726/b21125

Bibliographic information published by the **Deutsche Nationalbibliothek.**
The German National Library lists this publication in the German National Bibliography; detailed bibliographic data is available on the Internet at http://dnb.d-nb.de.

Cover design by Peter Lang Group AG

ISSN 2168-6432 (print)
ISBN 9781636674025 (paperback)
ISBN 9781636674063 (ebook)
ISBN 9781636674070 (epub)
DOI 10.3726/b21125

© 2023 Peter Lang Group AG, Lausanne
Published by Peter Lang Publishing Inc., New York, USA
info@peterlang.com - www.peterlang.com

All rights reserved.
All parts of this publication are protected by copyright.
Any utilization outside the strict limits of the copyright law, without the permission of the publisher, is forbidden and liable to prosecution.
This applies in particular to reproductions, translations, microfilming, and storage and processing in electronic retrieval systems.

This publication has been peer reviewed.

CONTENTS

Foreword for Leading With A Critical Spirit: New Strategies for Educational Leaders	vii
Acknowledgments	ix
Chapter 1 Rationalizing A Critical Definition of Educational Leadership	1
Chapter 2 The Call to Critical Educational Leadership: Anchoring, A Future Orientation, and Purpose	15
Chapter 3 Aligning The Elements of Critical African American Spirituality with the Leadership Project	29
Chapter 4 Critical Reflection and the Educational Leader's Unfinishedness	51
Chapter 5 Indicting Antediluvian Leadership	69
Chapter 6 The Conclusion of the Matter	83
References	95
Index	97

FOREWARD FOR LEADING WITH A CRITICAL SPIRIT: NEW STRATEGIES FOR EDUCATIONAL LEADERS

A radical, yet deeply spiritual favor for racial and social justice is needed now more than ever before in educational leadership. As I write this, educational leaders find themselves in precarious racial, social and political times. States are banning the teaching of Black History in Advanced Placement (AP) courses and authoring legislation to dismantle Diversity, Equity, and Inclusion (DEI) efforts across school districts. In addition, right-wing political groups are creating lies that Critical Race Theory is being taught in K-12 schools, and schools are experiencing one of the gravest racial backlashes in recent history. These and other dynamics have rapidly shifted the context of schooling, and specifically, educational leadership.

Despite this, Dr. Michael Dantley's work continues to be a prophetic beacon of radical hope in a way that transcends time. His writing tantalizes the intellect, energizes the soul, and ignites righteous indignation to fight for racial and social justice in a way that is unrivaled.

And *Leading with a Critical Spirit: New Strategies for Educational Leaders* (hereafter Leading with a Critical Spirit) is no different. *Leading with a Critical Spirit* is complex, vast, profoundly important, and its relevance is undeniable. The strategies that Dantley lays out in this book have the power to rupture popular, yet impotent paradigms and practices, transform schools, and make schools affirming, robust and life-giving institutions for Black youth.

The book that you're about to read is more than just a collection of words, theories, and postulations for educational leaders. It is a journey, a spiritual experience, and a glimpse into the radical possibilities of what schools can be and what educational leaders can do. However, this can only happen if educational leaders are daring enough to abandon the suggested structural-functionalist remedies and embrace what Dantley calls "the intangibles of educational leadership, those non-quantifiable or empirical aspects of leading such as coming to grips with one's ontology, critical reflection."

Leading with a Critical Spirit is a distillation of the many lessons and wisdom that Dr. Dantley has amassed as a classroom teacher, principal, dean, university provost and vice president for over more than four decades. Therefore, this book rejects quick fixes, magic bullets, and pre-packaged positivist solutions. Rather, it prophetically compels the reader to invest their entire selves into a critical practice that can be a catalyst for profound and lasting transformation.

In the pages that follow, you will find a rich tapestry of what educational leadership is, a redefinition of educational leadership for impact, and the prophetic, yet practical possibilities that Critical Spirituality can open up for educational leaders.

Leading with a Critical Spirit will challenge you to think deeply about your role in radically transforming schools as you wrestle with the beauty, complexities, and tensions of educational leadership with your entire being.

Whether you're an educational leader, professor, parent, or just someone who is committed to racial and social justice, I know this book will offer you something of tremendous value.

My hope is that by reading this book your spirit will be ignited, your intellect will be simulated, and that your practice will be transformed. And my promise is that you will be inspired, yet challenged to move beyond the "as is" to bring forth the "not yet."

So, I invite you, to join Dr. Michael Dantley and all of us who are ready to lead with a critical spirit, on this journey.

In solidary for justice,
Terrance Green, PhD
Austin, Texas
2023

ACKNOWLEDGMENTS

This book has been written through the inspiration and motivation of several people. My family, wife, Carol, our three children, Ryan Nichole, Cameron and Johnathan and our children-in-law, Sylvester, and Andrea, as well as our grandsons, Nicolas and Evan have been my support throughout this process. I owe them so much gratitude for their patience and constant encouragement.

Colleagues such as Dr. Denise Taliaferro-Baszile, and Dr. Derrick Brooms, and Dr. Waverly Duck provided consistent prodding to complete this work. I am grateful to the Senior Series Editor, Dr. Peter McLaren, for offering the opportunity to contribute to this significant work.

Finally, a powerful prayer warrior, Kathryn Burns-Sanders kept me, and this work covered in prayer and I will not forget her commitment to seeing me successfully complete this work. For Kathryn's prayers, I am exceptionally grateful.

· 1 ·

RATIONALIZING A CRITICAL DEFINITION OF EDUCATIONAL LEADERSHIP

This is a book on educational leadership. It is a treatise on critically divergent ways to define and think about leadership in education. This book proposes not only to provide definitions and multiple ways of thinking about leadership, but it also offers some stinging critique of the traditional ways of conceptualizing and therefore implementing educational leadership practices. Let me be clear, the book is more than an indictment of traditional notions of educational leadership but juxtaposes those historic and almost universally accepted assertions about leadership with critical perspectives that more genuinely enscence this human dynamic. My hope is for this book to do more than offer a critical lens through which to examine leadership and particularly educational leadership. As a result of this examination, I hope that this book does not resort to offering how-to edicts on leading educational sites. Differing from most books on educational leadership, this one runs the risk of seeing the potential efficacy of priming the leadership pump through an ephemeral catalyst. In fact, this book dares to assert that leadership can emanate from a spiritual epicenter whose dynamism is often left unnoticed and untouched by scholars and leadership practitioners. Traditionally, they abandon leadership to the rigid parameters of positivism, empiricism, and structural-functionalist theoretical frames.

Unashamedly and unabashedly, this book focuses attention on the implications, educational leadership grounded in a spiritual motif, may proffer. It dares to deconstruct a long-standing divide between the secular and the sacred and therefore founds a good deal of the discussion on educational leadership in the almost forbidden realm of spirituality and Black spirituality at that. It is often concluded that conversations about spirituality must be left to those frocked with religious vestments or at least to those who maintain some sacred divestment from secular ways of seeing the world. What I intend, however, through the pages of this book, is to articulate a comprehensive discussion of the role of critical spirituality in empowering educational leadership to matter in ways that are not the norm but, from my perspective, are essential.

For years, I have been fascinated with the subject of leadership. My desire has been not only to understand the very nature of leadership but also to embark upon a search as to how leadership can be a catalyst for democratization of our society. I have wondered and written about how leadership, and in this case, educational leadership, can have impact, to bring substantive, radical and socially just changes to our world. Of course, this is a tall order but leadership that has its foundation in spirituality, I contend, sees that order as not only doable but essential. Allow me to provide insight into my thinking.

If ever there were a serious need to articulate a more propitious and comprehensive definition of leadership, it is now. As I write this, the confluence of political lunacy with personal expediency that has emanated from the forty-fifth presidential administration occupies my thinking about leadership. I feel, only too poignantly, the tragedies of a supposed federal leadership that masterfully facilitated the deaths of countless thousands of people because of utter ignorance regarding the reality of the COVID pandemic. On top of this leadership fiasco, there are so many instances of persons carrying the title of leader, from the presidency of countries, governors and legislators, the presidencies of universities and corporations, to local heads of political, educational, and religious institutions, who believe that leadership is an autocratic and despotic operation. They believe that by executive fiat all that they are fantasizing about will come to pass. They are not constitutionally driven but are motivated by a narcissism that imagines ventures and enterprises that enhance their own aggrandizement. These functionaries see themselves as emperors. However, they are despots without clothes, clearly dismissing the fact that their observers, even without formal training in leadership theory, recognize their very poor efforts at perpetrating and propagating the leadership role. These men and women lack trustworthiness, integrity, or the essential leadership acumen to help those, whom they are purportedly leading, to trek paths of accomplishment, contribution, and self-fulfillment. These people are frauds and charlatans who have absolutely no motivation to positively impact anyone's life other than their own. They use their leadership position as a platform to spew supremacist propaganda, puffery and arguments that defy rationality and are bereft of an ounce of moral fiber.

The United States has vividly seen what leadership was not in the forty-fifth president. Allow me to qualify. Leadership that points to enhancing and improving the lives of those who are oppressed or who have been besieged by the systemic, societal forces that produce oppression, disenfranchisement, and imprisoning others in spaces of bondage and marginalization had not been the characteristic of the leadership the world had seen that emanated from the Oval Office and the U.S. Congress from 2016 to 2020.

The behaviors of the federal leaders jaundiced many on the productivity of leadership. It was seen as a vehicle for self-promotion or a way to placate their narcissistic pathology. I am aided in my discourse on the disdain for the forty-fifth presidential administration by an essay written by Chimamanda Ngozi Adichie (2021), in the book *The Matter of Black Lives: Writing from the New Yorker*, where she writes,

> The election of Donald Trump has flattened the poetry in America's founding philosophy: the country born from an idea of freedom is to be governed by an unstable, stubbornly uninformed, authoritarian demagogue. And in response to this there are people living in visceral fear, people anxiously trying to discern policy from bluster, and people kowtowing as though to a new king. Things that were recently pushed to the corners of America's political space-overt racism, glaring misogyny, and anti-intellectualism-are once again creeping to the center. (p. 99)

What is essential, at this time, because of the lingering effects of the forty-fifth administration, is the articulation of a leadership definition that will forge a comprehensive, strategic battle against the rising nihilism that has taken a very strong hold on the psyche of many in this nation.

The paucity of national leadership was so very evident during the time of the initial stages of the Coronavirus pandemic. Undoubtedly, an on-edge American public sorely needed inspiration, truthfulness, and the accurate communication of facts from all levels of leadership. However, what the American populace received, from several federal spokespersons and state and local officials, were lies and inaccurate, politicized information. Additionally, the awaiting public observed compliance with the multiple false narratives from some scientists and medical professionals, with those who had titular, political power. The medical professionals performed obeisance to those with governmental power even when the words coming out of those officials' mouths hardly approximated the truth. When we needed guidance, we received political posturing and speeches that portended presidential ennoblement. Indeed, in a word, the very idea of leadership suffered greatly through this past season of episodic buffoonery.

Because of the leadership debacle that had unfortunately caught the attention of the media, a much more useful definition of leadership is called for. What these current displays of leadership vacuum demonstrate is that people are easily duped by even a poorly designed leadership ruse. Additionally, the presence of a very poor disguise of national leadership leaves us clamoring for signs of leadership that forecast a dynamic future that will transcend the apocalyptic times we are currently experiencing. We are demonstrating how leadership really does matter.

I have penned the words of this book through the gnawing presence of a pathos that is engendered from an abiding agony over the lack of exemplary, United States, national, governmental leadership since 2016. Additionally, the morass of democratic leadership on the state-wide and local levels gives rise to more personal and public demands for leaders who embrace notions of justice and equity and the celebration of the humanity of all people. I fully admit that the broader social and political landscape that I am focusing on may cause some to wonder just how it impacts educational leadership practice in the local schoolhouse. Some may offer that these myriad societal challenges and issues that I am alluding to are not the essential foci of educational leadership. That assigning the solving of these dilemmas should be left, wisely, to the politicians, economists, and governmental bureaucrats. However, I would maintain that a major contributing influence on these people to whom some would assign the resolution of these issues have been their educational experiences. Part of the influences that have shaped their dispositions and opinions has been their engagement with their education. Their education, simply put, has been a major socializing agent that has helped them to form their predilections and even their political positions.

This book offers, without apology, that an educational leadership that forthrightly embraces the influences of world and national as well as local community issues is one that best situates learners to deal and indeed come to ameliorate the challenges, we, as a society, are facing. I am tipping my hand early in this text in asserting that educational leadership becomes effectual or productive only when it recognizes that what happens in schools is greatly impacted by what happens around them. Concomitantly, I assert that taking seriously into consideration environmental influences, through a critical theoretical lens, aligned with notions of African American spirituality, portends the possible transformation of the educational process and ultimately our society.

Please be patient with one more historical point. Again, Adichie helps me with this as she writes "that history gives both context and warning" (p. 101). The impeachment of Donald Trump twice in little over a year was further indication that a leadership malaise in this country existed. Additionally, my pathos, during the Trump administration, was birthed from the heart-wrenching reality that what was so very essential at that time, a forthright, inspiring, and visionary leadership from spaces where we've looked before and found it, could not afford us even a mere glimpse of behavior that vaguely resembled genuine leadership. There is a biblical passage, in the New Testament that recounts how Jesus lamented over the fact that the people had no leader. Christ's angst was birthed from the grievous reality that the people were without a shepherd. Even in his divinity, the importance of leadership for human beings was a fact that evoked sadness from Jesus when it was evident to him that this valuable treasure could not be found.

So, I write from anger blended with hope and from the compunction to present a definition of educational leadership that can be efficacious in setting the world on a new course. That is, an educational leadership that is fully cognizant of the contexts that are pleading for ways to successfully navigate the labyrinthine paths all kinds of national and international challenges are requiring. It is from this motivation that I dare to posit a definition of leadership that matters. Allow me to define educational leadership from my perspective, my history, my experiences, and my training.

Leadership is a complex interplay of elements, such as visioning, listening, influencing, guiding, communicating, collaborating, and delegating. It involves having the skill to inspire others to coalesce around a goal, objective, and vision that prove to be fulfilling and meaning-making for hopefully, everyone who would participate. Leadership is not clothed in raiment of perfection, infallibility, or condescension. But rather, leadership is the compilation of critical self-reflection, tempered self-confidence, and self-awareness. But that self-awareness is not simply for personal grandeur or profit. It is so that the leadership that results from such consciousness ignites an agenda that is disruptive. That is a leadership that provokes the disruption of spaces where asymmetric relations of power exist, where racist and supremacist behaviors are undergirded by extant and historical policies and procedures. Further, it is a leadership that offers hope where notions of a future sans the agents of dehumanization, marginalization, and disenfranchisement rule the day. Howard Thurman (1958) helps in recognizing the humanity of those who lead when he offers:

> The fact that a man can always be in error with reference to the things that he thinks he understands most clearly is an ever-present reminder of human frailty. It is a challenge to humility even in the presence of one's deepest convictions ... We are all creatures of limitation and it behooves us to recognize this fact at every point. (pp. 21–22)

I have penned this book fully realizing my creature nature of limitation. My perspectives as well as my experiences limit me to their implications, their influences, and their interpretations. I readily admit that. However, the claim for a more humane and moral demonstration of leadership in education emanating from multiple voices is real. And so, it is from that motivation that I write this book.

Additionally, I author this book from my years of being an educational and religious leader, from teaching many, many graduate courses in educational leadership at the university level, over 47 years of pastoring a congregation and from years of serious reflection and critical contemplation on the inherent vicissitudes and nuances that are alive and well in the practice of educational leadership. Though in distinct venues, with their own unique cultures, I have found similarities in the undergirding thinking and moral grounding or principled framework essential to sustaining leadership in both educational as well as religious settings. However, this book will only focus on leadership in school or education spaces.

My perspectives have been peppered by the theoretical positions of several scholars; some who are not known for their scholarly contributions to leadership theory, including Cornel West, Howard Thurman, Ta-Nehesi Coates, James Cone, bell hooks, Eddie Glaude, Michael Eric Dyson, and Paulo Freire. Others, who have devoted their intellectual muscle to developing the investigation of the interplay of those who lead and those who are led, have also been influential in my musings on this subject. Both groups of scholars have tremendously contributed to my thinking about leaders and followers. And even that binary construction, that of leading and following, has been disrupted and deconstructed throughout my wrangling with what it means to lead.

When one adopts a critical, more just and democratically based way to think about leadership, that binary of leader and led is troubled by its inherent notions of dehumanizing and marginalizing behaviors. Such behaviors are often grounded in racism, sexism, classism, ableism, homophobia, queerphobia (Smith, 2020) and xenophobia, only to name a few. So, I unashamedly admit that for me, leadership becomes bereft of genuine meaning when the binary of leader and led is left inconvenienced.

I have adopted the critical theoretical lens for writing the book as the way to examine leadership practice. The critical way of seeing the world of leadership is a radical approach that gives primacy to issues of democracy, justice, and disrupting hegemonic social and political constructions. It calls for the identification of systemic structures that perpetuate marginalization based on racial, social class, gender, sexual, and other markers of identity. A critical way of viewing the world is often delineated in fields such as Critical Race, Black Crit, Feminist, Womanist, and Queer Theory, all of which take the position that organizations operate from inherent and thriving systems of domination. They perpetuate the efficacy of white male privilege and their self-congratulating ways of seeing the world and they therefore ignore or at best subjugate other oppositional ways of viewing the world in which leadership is undoubtedly grounded.

Colleen Capper (2019) outlines six key principles of critical theory. These include, "acknowledge and relieve suffering and oppression; critique education's perpetuation and disruption of power; reunite facts with values with a goal of social justice praxis; power between the oppressor and oppressed; power disrupted via communication from equal participation; and leadership is political" (p. 69–71). The compilation of the six principles will assist me in contouring the argument I will make where leadership matters particularly in forging an agenda of justice, equity, and anti-discriminatory leadership behavior. Critical theory aligned with African American leadership (Marable, 1998; Walters & Smith, 1999) as well as African American spirituality and tenets of critical spirituality (Dantley, 2005) will also found the arguments presented in making the formidable conclusion that leadership matters.

I also write this book as an African American man who has had to navigate and contend with the challenges of being *the first*. Those challenges were inbred because of the systemic cultures of the institutions in which I have served that have been grounded in racist and marginalizing stereotypes. I take some blame, however, for the creation of these challenges because of my own sense of needing to achieve and prove myself worthy of standing in these positions of leadership as *the first*. Being the first African American in a position of leadership, however, is replete with both extraordinary and underwhelmed expectations by those who are participants in this panoply of relationships. You are at once ensconced with the Sidney Poitier's celebrated pedigree, as in the film, *Guess Who's Coming to Dinner*, where Poitier comes to the house of his white fiancé as a Harvard trained physician. While at the same time, being the first African American in a leadership position, subjects you either overtly or surreptitiously to being saddled with colonial, postcolonial, antebellum, Civil War, lynching mob, Reconstruction, Jim Crow, hoses and dogs, Edmund Pettus Bridge, white supremacist, notions of your supposed, ingrained ineptitude and inability to successfully perform leadership functions. The duality is a built-in reality that comes with your positionality of being Black.

I hasten to offer succinctly but also emphatically that positionality is almost everything. It colors our perspectives while our perspectives concomitantly color our positionality. For instance, it is impossible for me to lead from an authentic space if I subject myself to operating in the pathology of many people's commitment to colorblindness. Such a way to obfuscate color for some people, assuages the self-inflicted guilt they accrue from the racist positions others who see race as being negative and foreboding adopt. Colorblindness becomes a vehicle to articulate a sense that by not seeing color, those people who embrace this dismissive idea, have risen above those who harbor the indictment that being a person of color comes with rancor, malevolence, villainous behavior, and essential social ostracism. I am taken with Patricia Hill Collins' (2013) perspective on colorblindness. She offers,

> The rush to embrace the ideal of colorblindness fosters a shift away from the types of racially explicit language of anti-racist politics that facilitated political action. Racism didn't magically go away just because we refuse to talk about it. Rather, overt racial language is replaced by covert racial euphemisms that reference the same phenomena ... Everyone knows what these terms mean and if they don't, they quickly figure it out. (p. 35)

Colorblindness is not a banal, inconsequential dynamic. Abnegating my racial and cultural heritage and pretending that my position as a Black, educated, Christian, married, man has absolutely nothing to do with my views of leadership, makes absolutely no sense and diminishes the integrity of my actions as a leader. What is significant is this commutative relationship of positionality and position in assisting us, as African Americans, to navigate this leadership space. Intriguing is the notion that because of our proclivities, perspectives, principles, and personalities, we have been placed in leadership assignments. However, we cannot dismiss the social and political accouterment that also plays prominently in how we are received, perceived, placated, or persecuted as we carry out our leadership responsibilities.

So, this book dares to grapple with a host of complexities. It looks at leadership from multiple lenses. It will challenge some traditional notions of leadership and will offer ways to wrestle with some of the more ethereal elements that are often left unexamined when leadership behavior is under investigation. So, let's begin with a personal reflection.

There was a rectangular sign, trimmed in red and white, posted on the back of the door in my university office that read, "Speak the truth in love and anger." I recall handwriting that sign, with a black permanent marker, at the beginning of an academic year when I was adopting those words as the imprimatur for my leadership behavior, as dean, during the following 12 months. There was something both motivating as well as captivating about the coalescence of love and anger serving as the descriptors for my leadership behavior. The two bordered on being a binary. Hoverer I was not actually concerned by the potential bifurcation, behaving inspired by love and anger simultaneously, may have evoked. I was not concerned that what could appear to be two emotions that had the potential to represent each other's antithesis could provoke pathology in my behavior. Nor was I troubled by the fact that such pathology would leave me betwixt and between. Quite honestly, I have come to accept the reality of living betwixt and between and embrace that certainty as a diurnal fact of my life.

All leaders who are honest will admit that their lives habitually reside in the morass of the certainty of uncertainty and that they are the habiture of contested volitions, intentions, and their own predilections, all of the time. Leaders who feign confidence in their strategies for decision-making and seldom, if ever second-guessing themselves, are doing their best to perpetuate a leadership caricature that genuinely does not exist. Each day, leaders face dilemmas and challenges that will cause them to conjure up multiple resolutions, each seeming to be more or less effectual than the other. Daily, leaders meet their responsibilities within a context of competing priorities and contentions, both internally and exogenously. Leaders fully embrace the fact that their challenges are not resolved through the application of some theory or even through the treasures of their previous experiences. Each day the very hard work of leadership is getting people to move with you even when you are unsure about the path and definitely uncertain of what lies at the end of the chosen path. Almost every day, a leader has to rekindle the resolve to move ahead even in a space replete with ambiguity and incongruity. It is for these reasons that leadership demands one to know oneself and to accept one's consistent and so often tenuous position of being in a constant state of dissonance.

Leadership does not occur in a frictionless environment. It happens within the interplay of personal, institutional, and societal assumptions about its definition and behaviors. To therefore courageously ground leadership in the behaviors of speaking truth and anger contextualizes this social, political, and indeed spiritual dynamic in an area that marginalizes traditional, positivistic thinking about how leadership genuinely matters. Though externally impacting, leadership finds its source within the very depth of an individual's personality. It emanates from the core, the space in the individual that yearns for making meaning, connection, and transformation.

What I allowed to surface in the writing of that sign that August afternoon, was the reality of my self-reflection. As a leader, I was determined to speak. I was determined not to be silent nor allow myself to be silenced. I was determined to have a voice, a distinct voice, my voice that emanated from my lived experiences and purview and to articulate unabashedly my voice on whatever it was that I observed. It had become clear to me that despite how I had internalized some bastardized, self-deprecating notion of humility and some warped sense of being gracious, that not speaking, remaining reticent, swallowing my words in order to remain sanguine was hindering possibilities of essential reform that could be birthed simply through my speaking.

In the nascent of the academic year, I made the decision to be counted. I had adopted what Howard Thurman (1951), in his book *Deep Is the Hunger*, calls developing "the climate within" (p. 8). This was an act of courage because there were consequences that accompanied the articulation of my voice. No doubt, abstaining from maintaining silence could result in the presence of antiphonal voices of opposition. There was the great possibility of negatively impacting the self-perceptions of others as my voice could compel them to interrogate their own positions, to question their predispositions and to deconstruct the foundations upon which they had built a lifetime of belief systems and their accompanying behaviors.

I have called this inner-work and then the vocal articulation of my thinking a courageous act because as Derrick Bell (2002), writes in *Ethical*

Ambition: Living a Life of Meaning and Worth, courage and risk-taking are accomplished in a discursive context of fear. Bell asserts,

> The consequence feared might be minor ("If I say what I think, he'll be angry ..."), but it must be real. You can feel at risk because your sense of self is threatened, or your job, or you ego, or the happiness of a loved one. The consequence might even seem of little importance to somebody else ("So they don't promote you, so you'll go work somewhere else, big deal"), but the consequence must seem real to you. (p. 41)

Developing the climate within is one of those essential elements of a leader's growth that is just as important as understanding decision-making processes, legal and budgetary matters, group dynamics, and organizational structures. Without attending to one's climate within leaves leaders indigent of the wherewithal not only to operationalize leadership behaviors but also to feel confident that they are doing so from an authentic and integrated self. My fear is that so often we lead having ignored or abandoned our climate within. We behave professionally as if what we are engaging personally has no impact on our leadership practice. My desire is for educational leaders to place in a secondary position the technical demands of leading to the primacy of deliberately attending to their climate within. Allow me to provide some preliminary thoughts about leadership and one's spirit especially since the climate within can most certainly be funded by one's spirit.

I have come to fully understand that leadership is a spiritual endeavor. To limit the work of leadership to a technical or intellectually driven enterprise reduces it to a mechanical device that actually does not and will not work. Leadership encompasses the motivation and inspiration of individuals to coalesce around a vision designed to move that collective to a more desired future. No doubt were most people to be polled, they would celebrate leadership characteristics such as consistency, empiricism, data-driven decision-making and other objective ways to lead an organization. But they would also offer that the context within which all those empirical strategies are executed, must nonetheless, be one that celebrates and prioritizes the nature of and care for human beings. It must be a context grounded in even a modicum of understanding of human motivation, those ways in which we are inspired and challenged to pursue new vistas and frontiers. It must be a leadership that resonates with and celebrates one's climate within. The human element is the only facet of the organization that really is pivotal to its success. Leadership is all about people. It may pronounce commitments to a bottom line or the significance of profit or net new revenue. However, none of this can be accomplished without people who are inspired to make it happen. None of this happens unless the people in the organization have invested in how the bottom line reached by the organization makes meaning and significance for their lives, individually and collectively. Additionally, there will be those in the organization who will pursue how the bottom line not only impacts them personally but also has residual impact on communities and other institutions that may be in the direct path. There is a substantive quid pro quo that must be realized by those in the organization before they will wholeheartedly commit to its vision and mission. Only an individual who has taken the time and the effort to develop their climate within will have the wherewithal to lead, understanding the tremendous prerequisite and significance of the human commitment and the spiritual acknowledgment of others' climate within.

The plan for this book comes with the desire to blend scholarly and pragmatic lenses to the practice of leadership. This allows me to align the major epistemological foundations that undergird the notions of leadership that have greatly impacted my life as a practitioner and scholar. The plan also takes a courageous leap to lay out definitions and effectual characteristics for the field of educational institutions in both Pre-K-12 and higher educational settings. In many ways, the lessons to be posited here are synonymous for both worlds. Both have been grievously guilty of perpetuating a discriminatory marginalization of those whom society has positioned as the persons to be systemically disenfranchised. Concomitantly, both have endorsed mechanisms that celebrate the silence and offering deference and obeisance to those systemic machinations that oppress and militate against justice and equality.

In so many ways, scholarship has nourished my practice and practice has been the vitamin supplement for my scholarship. The writing of this book comes after a commitment to, as much as possible, resolving the innate competition and juxtaposing of both worlds of my life, education, and the church, to a point of relative stasis or a modicum of equilibrium. Such equanimity results from at least recognizing the significance and the nurturing impact of both influences.

To do this, we will explore, in some depth the elements of African American leadership as mentioned earlier. The spiritual dimension that undergirds critical self-reflection, tempered self-confidence and self-awareness will also be focused upon within the pages of this book. Critical theoretical perspectives will undergird the book's messages. In fact, scholarship I have written before on critical spirituality will serve as a founding pillar for this work. So, scholars of leadership as well as practitioners should find succor, challenge, and accountability in the words on these pages.

Those persons who have an interest in leadership, who are training to become leaders and who are leaders themselves in educational spaces and those who know that their authentic, integrated self must be the one who leads in these diverse venues are the audience for this work.

· 2 ·

THE CALL TO CRITICAL EDUCATIONAL LEADERSHIP: ANCHORING, A FUTURE ORIENTATION, AND PURPOSE

There are several givens, that were mentioned earlier, that coalesce to attempt to define leadership. And may I quickly add that those givens are highly fluid. For it is not hyperbole to admit that leadership is a conundrum. It is not an easily defined, scientifically proven phenomenon. For anyone to believe that leadership can be reduced to formulas of quadrants and measurable behaviors demonstrates that the person has completely missed out on the inherent complexities, the inexplicable nuances and the, what must be termed, ethereal occurrences that name this relational dynamic among human beings. Even when one dares to identify or to name leaders, the litany that follows really has no monolithic theme. There is no compendium of traits or characteristics that is consistently and irrevocably present in leadership's DNA.

As we consider and articulate the composite acts or behaviors a leader executes, were we honest, we would have to admit that not all leaders execute these behaviors, not all leaders have the capacity to engage in these behaviors, and not all these behaviors are necessarily, qualitatively moral, or humane and serve as excellent models of the leadership moniker. This statement sounds as if the characteristics of moral or humane are unequivocal descriptors of leadership. And though I have just admitted that there is no one list of qualifiers that names leadership accurately, I, nonetheless, strongly believe that critical educational leadership is specifically grounded in the pursuit of greater demonstrations of democracy. Therefore, ethical, moral, and humane thinking and behaviors must motivate educational leadership practices.

Additionally, our admission would have to include that those deemed to be exemplar leadership actions, often emanate from hallmarked and highlighted performances that the media has celebrated. These prized actions of these named or highlighted leaders have caused something to happen, so much so that a critical mass of individuals has embraced the idea or the project and have submitted their efforts to getting it done. And because of the successful accomplishment of these efforts, the person who facilitated the process is hailed as an effective leader. Perhaps the honored notions of rugged individualism, the celebrated portrayals of the frontiersman and other misogynistic displays of male dominance have fed into these perverse ideas of leadership. So, is the person who gets something done a leader? Is the person who gets others to get something done a leader? Or is there much more to this that only leadership scholars explore, and others find unnecessary and a complete waste of time? I would hope that because you are engaging with this text that you at least find the exploration of the subject of leadership intriguing. Perhaps not riveting but at least interesting.

Let's return for a moment to the spurious exercise of creating a litany of leadership characteristics. Lest you believe that I am indulging in self-contradictory pronouncements it is essential that I clearly write that my perspectives on educational leadership are so much more than the technical practices of managing a school building. Indeed, educational leadership, from my vantage point, is all about facilitating a learning environment to see broader social implications for the work that takes place in that school setting. A critical grounding of educational leadership forces notions of leadership to be focused on just how schooling is a major institution for propagating democratic principles, anti-racist perspectives, and humanitarian projects. That means that the usual list of leadership attributes so often negates these broader purposes and perhaps sees them as the responsibility of other societal institutions.

So often that list of traditional managerial traits is full of characteristics that are generally believed to be possessed by men and specifically white men at that. Those characteristics include such elements as courage, toughness, boldness, aggression, perseverance, and others that have been generally relegated to historically male descriptors. Years ago, the Great Man Theory of leadership included such ridiculous personal characteristics as height and athletic ability and even being good-looking. The complexities inherent in naming leadership qualities must be, in my mind, deeply appreciated and must also deliberately eschew what have been historically cast as being typically masculine characteristics. Such concepts as being inspirational, insightful, communicative, and collaborative must be included in what I would call a comprehensive list of leadership attributes. It is most beneficial to ascribe non-gender-based characteristics to educational leadership. It is even a lucrative practice to refrain from labeling leadership attributes as being hard or soft. Using such nomenclature continues the sexualization of leadership practice and can in subtle ways serve as the foundation for propagating behaviors that marginalize and promote gender and other identity oppression. Additionally, leadership characteristics may emanate from the nature of the organization or the challenge that requires the leadership performance. Indeed, a leader operates from an arsenal of resources that comes to bear given the set of circumstances that color the institution or given the work that is purported to be accomplished.

At the time of my writing this book, Congressman John Lewis, the valiant Civil Rights warrior died. Deserved accolades and commendations memorialized his life. Many eulogists attributed the title of leader to Congressman Lewis. They cited his work as a young man with SNCC, the Student Nonviolent Coordinating Committee, the young people's arm of the burgeoning Civil Rights Movement in the 1960s. They remembered his speech at the March on Washington and recalled how the elders in the movement wanted him to turn down the temperature of his remarks to a tepid pitch. Yet he announced with even greater fervor the impatience Black folk possessed for waiting to finally live with equal rights and justice as U.S. citizens. He is heralded for leading the march on Bloody Sunday, across the Edmund Pettus Bridge in Selma, Alabama, the march for voting rights for African American people. Congressman John Lewis has been proclaimed to have been the moral conscience of the U.S. Congress. Yet, those who have eulogized him have offered that he was a gentle man; he was a man of reason, strategic diplomacy and one who inspired hope and perseverance for those who were fighting the necessary fight, causing good trouble, for equality and justice, even when opposed by formidable oppression.

By several standards and criteria, Congressman Lewis has been called a leader. However, there is something markedly different about his style. There is something, almost indefinable about his leadership behavior. His behavior disrupted the hegemonic definitions of leadership. There was an aura about him that in many ways reified notions of leadership. Indeed, he got things done but without a lot of bravado. He got things done but through a manner that eschewed ostentation and limelight. His moves were calculated with passion and precision and punctuated with purpose and principle. These are not normal notions that catalog leadership behavior. These may be skills that have traditionally been underplayed as essential puzzle pieces to the leadership enigma. What Congressman Lewis' leadership did was to heighten the conflation of complexity and convolution of what we have come to name as leadership. Michael Denzel Smith (2020) in his book *Stakes Is High: Life after the American Dream*, opens a poignant discussion on leadership and notions of power that he offers are finding themselves appropriately under question and pointed examination. Smith writes,

> Men have become so enraptured by their own definition of power, one steeped in the ideology of domination coercion, manipulation, violence, and thievery (all undemocratic forms of rule), that they fail to take note of the forms of power building around them based on cooperation, compassion healing, and a shared interest in each other's survival. When men meet this kind of power, they are stunned, largely because they have never been tasked with conceiving of a world in which their own dominance was not taken as a given. (pp. 114–115)

The narcissism that has marred men in positions of power like Donald Trump has released a deeper nihilism throughout society that a leadership style can most definitely assuage. However, such a leadership style must be completely antithetical to the one Trump and his minions have used. A leadership style that dares to celebrate compassion and collaboration, care and cooperation can see monumental benefits in manifesting hope and positive expectations throughout society. These are indeed behaviors we learned in kindergarten and have successfully sustained healthy, amicable relationships ever since. A word of caution, however. This is not a leadership without critique. It is exactly because the evidence of asymmetric relations of power must be exposed through critique that other leadership practices grounded in patriarchy, heteronormativity, and American exceptionalism may be replaced by this new genre of leadership. Given that reality, I will attempt to articulate some notions of educational institutional leadership especially grounded in a critical Black motif that will potentially assist us in more effectively leading educational institutions and organizations. Such an articulation will celebrate the leadership model Congressman John Lewis has left behind for us.

If we return to the loosely tethered notions that coalesce to attempt to define leadership, we will concede that there are the social and institutional vestments that dress the scaffolding of leadership. These often present a varnished view of institutions as if they are without spot or wrinkle and are not guilty of perpetuating hegemony of evil and oppression. That is a very strident accusation, but it really represents the context within which many institutional, including educational systems' bottom lines are achieved. Often there is very little thought about the welfare of the individuals laboring in institutions. They are viewed as a means to an end. Highlighting the climate within is hardly ever considered as leaders make decisions to move the institution forward toward its supposed bottom line. In fact, Cornel West (1988) articulates very clearly how workers sell their competencies to organizations for institutional profit. This transaction comes without real concern or care for the worker. As the prize that sustains the eye, which is the institution's profit, the financial aggrandizement of the organization.

West further explicates the notion of victimization, as he argues that many human beings experience what he calls "thick forms of victimization" (p. 113). It is West's purpose to speak to corporate oppressive practices by, "promoting protracted and principled struggles against types of personal despair, intellectual dogmatism, and socioeconomic oppression that foster communities of hope" (p. 113). It may seem oxymoronic to argue that these personal protracted struggles of personal despair and intellectual dogmatism enfold into communities of hope. However, a leader who embraces these challenges as prominent pieces of an educational site's personality will expend energy in behaving in both professional and personal ways to grapple with these challenges. In so doing, what Ron Heifetz (1999) calls a holding environment is erected and morphs into a community of hope. It becomes a space where candor, misgivings, apprehensions, aversion, and all nature of responses to life are welcome and are perceived as the lens through the work of educating is viewed. It certainly is the concept of communities of hope that underlies the role of spirituality, another ingredient that is hardly ever noted as a preferred element of leadership practice.

It is this commitment to what West calls principled and protracted struggle that provides the stage for spirituality and leadership to perform their sonorous duet. Perhaps it is terribly unrealistic to adorn an organization with the moniker of being a community of hope. Living up to such a titular expectation is almost impossible for most capitalist-driven institutions to achieve. However, educational institutions can certainly become spaces where the creation of communities of hope may be both internally and externally forged. Implied in the birthing of these communities of hope are the pangs of West's protracted struggles catalyzed by leadership visions drenched in the effervescence of justice, equity, and purer forms of democracy. As important is the ethereal presence that mollifies as well as encourages decisions and steps leaders take every single day. It is that spiritual reality of leadership that grounded leaders like Congressman John Lewis, that we will now consider.

Much is misunderstood about spirituality. It is often burdened with manifold definitions and explanations. In fact, some would argue that leadership and spirituality are exogamous and the oxymoronic nature of forging such an alignment defies logical or rational reckoning. However, the significance of spirituality and not necessarily religion in a leader's repertoire is manifold. Those who base knowledge and indeed truth based on empirical evidence may have difficulty in wrapping their minds around notions of the spirit. It is when we lock ourselves into a positivistic and structural-functional frame of reference, that we then force ourselves into a psychic prison that limits our epistemological frame to only that which can be proven through empirical design. The spirit, however, cannot be evidenced through such a mechanism. And yet, the spirit is real. Our spirit is effectual.

Please embrace early on, the fact that for many African Americans, spirituality is an essential lens through which our worldview is created, how our interactions are cultivated and how our decisions are grounded. There is an undeniable reliance upon one's spirit in not just religious endeavors but also in everyday, mundane as well as momentous matters in our lives. Essentially, for many African Americans, our spirit does not enjoy a separate existence from all other facets of our lives. Our spirit is intertwined and is mutually influenced and influential on many aspects of how we live every day.

Joseph White and James Cones III (1999) in *Black Man Emerging: Facing the Past and Seizing a Future in America*, go to great lengths to delineate the character and impact of the spirit on our lives. They argue that "spirituality ... is symbolized by a vibrant belief that a spiritual force acts as a connecting link to all life and all beings" (p. 118). White and Cones maintain that spirituality and of course one's embracing of spirituality, is the motivating force for achieving human potential. The authors compel us to celebrate not only the physical and cerebral portions of our existence but also the part of us that connects us with something greater than ourselves.

Spirituality compels us to grapple, through self-reflection and an internal environmental scan, with what it is that creates meaning for us and an essential highlighting of the ways in which we are making substantive contributions to our world. Spirituality is much more than our possessing the riches of self-efficacy, though that is one of the profits from our spiritual wrestling. It forces us to use our self-efficacy to understand a distinct existential element of leadership. That essential element is our *calling*. I submit that included in a leadership calling those matters is also a commitment to justice and equity. With justice and equity at the epicenter of one's calling, also comes the dismantling of those systemic appurtenances that maintain inequity, disenfranchisement, and human oppression in the organizations that we lead. Let us delve into the tenets of calling to examine this existential element of spiritual leadership.

Leaders who embrace the fact that calling is a spiritual function already see that their work is beyond the confines of technical and bureaucratic tedium. Calling is about the sense that purpose and intention are pivotal facets of a leader's work. This teleological element of leadership raises the exercise of leadership from the technical mechanics to the lofty and yet, simultaneously the pragmatism that makes leading through one's spirit efficacious.

Calling is a spiritual phenomenon that supersedes individual desire. Calling prompts the creation of vision and overwhelms the natural penchant toward doing work simply for personal gain. Calling is captivating. It embodies an idea, a concept, and a future that is relentless in getting one's attention. It provokes sleeplessness and invokes incessant attention paid to it. Calling is almost inescapable. It dominates, for many people, their consciousness because with calling comes a sense of restrained focus and perspective. Calling is aggressive in its intention to become the attention-grabbing direction for an individual. It has a way of positioning ego gratification in a space that usurps the intrinsic need for self-fulfillment by the need to serve a higher purpose. Calling requires an antiphonal response. And the positive response is often coupled with an accurate sense of personal inadequacy and unfinishedness. This antiphonal response lays bare the human being's awareness of their limitations, the enormity of the leadership task and the demand for resources that may indeed surpass the ordinary. This call and response signify time spent in critical self-reflection where a sense of challenge tempered by a self-inflicted castigation for even imagining such leadership exploits are in a sympathetic rhythm with one another. The one is not more pronounced than the other. The beat of one is no more distinct than the other. Both harmonize to make the leadership sound genuine and authentic. But the calling, without physical or natural nascent, ignites one's spirit with duty, purpose, vision, and intention.

Inherent in calling, that is this sense of an internal necessity and compunction to lead, this fulfilling of one's raison d'etre, is the additional understanding that calling is the impetus for leading. The existential nature of calling includes three components: *anchoring, a future orientation*, and *purposive motivation* or *intention*.

Without a spiritual grounding, a leader is bereft of the benefit of anchoring. Anchoring is that characteristic of a leader's behavior that promotes sustainability, perseverance, and commitment. Leaders are forever facing challenges that are loaded with stress and often have the potential to cause anxiety and exceptional levels of frustration. Because leadership is a "peopled phenomenon" the moods and behaviors of those who are impacted by leaders' actions as well as the very presence of oppositional thinking or alternative perceptions, while being organizationally, exceptionally healthy, may try the mettle and commitment of leaders if they are not anchored. Leaders themselves must face their own moods and shifting attitudes and often make decisions grounded in these shifting sands. However, anchoring causes leaders to juxtapose their attitudes and thinking with their embrace of their work as a calling. This self-reflection guides leaders to position their current predisposition along with those whom they are leading in a broader context. The hope is that repositioning brings leaders back to the fundamental reasons they are in positions of leadership and settles them to see these moments as a part of the course they are required to traverse. Leading in the context of the pandemic, COVID-19 and the worldwide protests stemming from the killings of George Floyd, Breanna Taylor, Amahad Arbery and Rayshard Brooks are all monumental tests of a leader's calling and specifically a leader's anchoring. There is no doubt that the confluence of social injustice and systemic racism colors the context within which educational leaders must work. Undoubtedly, educational leaders' wrangling with these serious matters, are not given the luxury to lead without the influence of these monumental events and the leaders' visceral responses to them. Further, when the demonstrations are over and the media no longer finds this work worthy of attention, there is still the residual from these times that will contour relationships and organizational structures for years to come. The aftereffects of this season of protest and calls for universal systemic change will have significant impact, hopefully for a long, long time.

Simply stated, leading is not easy. While leadership is not easy, human beings nonetheless exercise it. And within the very make-up of human beings are apprehensions, predilections, nerves, and buttons that can be plucked and pushed when model ways to respond, textbook scripted responses may not suffice. And it is most certainly then when anchoring gains its paramount importance. Without a consistent check-in with one's calling, leaders may be prone to throw in the towel and acquiesce to those challenging forces that are always facing them.

Anchoring also must be the prescription when Black leaders become consistently sickened by the racist microaggressions perpetrated by white people who see themselves as innocent, innocuous, well-meaning advocates for social justice. It is almost anathema how often social justice rhetoric and bureaucratic behavior exist in a structural space but indeed, as feuding neighbors. With the recent murders of Black citizens by white police, institutions have responded to the calls for an end to anti-Black racism with knee-jerk actions designed to color the institution temporarily in a Nubian hue. All the while, these suddenly well-intentioned institutions are not taking the time to strategically consider what, other than for the first-time recognizing Juneteenth or creating yet another task force whose white paper deigns to provide sudden answers to years of institutional history where supremacist, colonizing policies and procedures have ruled the day, should be constructed.

Anchoring is tested when Black leaders reach the incessant boiling point where continual disregard and constant disrespect have been the diurnal regimen for their existence in the organizational structure. You are a leader as are your white colleagues, but they are personally consulted about organizational concerns. Their brains are picked before major decisions are made and subsequently announced to you. You are positionally at the table but in essence you are the spook who sits at the table and not deemed to bring a significant contribution to the workings of the organization. So, the strength of a leader's anchoring is perpetually tested through the onslaught of racist microaggressions, racist macroaggressions, and other disenfranchising, institutional and interpersonal practices. Clearly, the monumental test Black leaders face is the inevitability where anchoring must have a sonorous presence to contend with and often work around the racist machinations of systems within which Black leaders must operate. We are advised to present certain behaviors in the face of anti-Black racism that not only placate supremacist intentions but also assuage the discomfort calling out such actions might cause the white people perpetuating them. The juxtaposition between the plantation context and the work to be done keeps the leader in a tug-of-war that only anchoring has the wherewithal to settle.

The second component of calling is the prominence, in a leader's thinking, of a future orientation. Inherent in an orientation that is not sutured to the present nor hopelessly tethered to the past, is a perspective that celebrates possibilities of the future. In fact, this outlook bears a very close resemblance to embracing a prophetic mindset about the culture and the conditions of the organization. The prophetic or future orientation can be couched in one of two categories. These two categories are assimilation or reconstruction. The critical analysis that is a part of the prophetic frame or the frame that calls for reconstruction will do everything to dismantle the systems and practices that accommodate assimilationist thinking. While the assimilationist perspective offers that the status quo is working. There is nothing to be amended in the way the organization operates. To the assimilationist, there are years of proven success that the organization enjoys and continuing in this vein is the only lucrative way to build the future. The culture of the organization is steadfast and immovable. All who would enter this organization would be required to become immersed in the extant culture, to fit in, to perpetuate its vision and mission without question and therefore, when falling in line, will not suffer anomie or cognitive dissonance. Within this notion of the prophetic, I need to re-emphasize, is included a systematic analysis and critique of an organization's structures and actions that marginalize and even minimize equity and purer forms of democratic practice. The whole idea of this kind of stringent critique is to portend, given the appropriate leadership, an organization creating and sustaining a community of hope. Such a community of hope is destined to set right societal wrongs that have been the progeny of the capitalist profiteering the organization has historically enjoyed.

The acrid critique from the prophetic assessment evaluates every fiber of the institutional fabric that has shrouded the inequitable machinations the organization has displayed throughout its existence. It is a critique that carefully and microscopically looks for the viruses that have been at the very foundation of the organization's malaise. The critique leaves no stone unturned when looking for procedural, programmatic and policy malfeasance. The basis of the community of hope is to engender an organization that will work to see racial, gender, sexual, class, ethnic and religious injustice, practiced throughout society, annihilated in a wholesale way.

The prophetic practice requires the type of candid organizational introspection that welcomes and celebrates self-critique and resultant action. It is the formulation of the actions that push the organization into the realization of the calling's future orientation. Inherent in this future orientation, grounded in a prophetic frame, is what Cornel West (1988) calls moral action. The character of the future orientation finds its vestments in the actions leaders take in assessing theirs and their organization's sincere commitment to promote this moral action. According to West, "moral action is based on a broad, robust prophetism that highlights systemic social analysis of the circumstances under which tragic persons struggle" (p. x.). Indeed, the future of the organization is not based solely on traditional notions of vision and mission. Rather, the future is envisioned after a careful and critical analysis of the systemic machinery that propagates behaviors that marginalize and capitalize on the veiled acts that rest on the tragic individuals either ignoring or not knowing the multiple ways they are being used for an oppressive organization's lucrative bottom line. A designated future without a critical evaluation of the historical roots of the past and the recognition that the vestiges of that history are still alive and well in the present, with their staunch commitment to remain in the future, simply cannot occur when the prophetic, critical work frames the leader's agenda.

It is important to note that this portion of the prophetic labor of a leader, the critical analysis, amounts to castigating its structures and those who built and sustain them. However, it is the exposing of these systemic contrivances that will assist in founding the future of the organization on a rock of transparency, accountability, the deconstruction of the oppressive mystique and the hope for a more just and democratic agenda for the organization's purpose and mission. It is particularly in the prophetic move of critical analysis that the leader must consistently call upon anchoring. A leader who is anchored in the leadership calling will require the organizational analytical exercise, will weather its residuals, and will implement the results from this work. This demands a stalwart commitment to the betterment of the organization and its future. If the future is to become one bereft of those policies and practices that have perpetuated racism, white supremacy, sexism, homophobia, ableism, or any other disenfranchised identity marker, then this incisive examination of the inner working of the organization is essential. Otherwise, the same, worn wardrobe the organization has been wearing for decades remains the cloak and even the shroud for its future.

Equally as impactful, through the prophetic gaze, is the presence of an imagination that dares to paint a bold future on the canvas of the educational institution. The future orientation is supported by the results of the critical analysis that works to establish a foundation for the future, replete with a candid assessment of the organization's miscreant behavior in its lack of maintaining a justice agenda. Additionally, as important however, is the celebration of those organizational practices that have taken the justice motif seriously. This demands a critical analysis of the ways the institution has made landmark decisions that focus on policies and procedures that bear the burden of deconstructing oppressive institutional practices. If these substantive events have taken place, then they deserve to be honored and used to establish the foundation for the future of the institution. The future is saturated in an articulated hope by leaders, who have undergone the significant work of the critical analysis. It emanates from a proclamation that the organization possesses all the ingredients to create a community of hope that rests in an agenda to engage forthrightly with anti-Black racism, white supremacy and the multitude of other marginalizing schemes that have been either boldly or clandestinely energized through the organization's structures, policies, culture, and behaviors.

We have explored the first two components of calling, anchoring and a future orientation and now we will engage in what I call purposive motivation or intention. Earlier, I explained how a calling places a parameter around our thinking and aligns us with exploits and missions that require us to behave in proactive ways while simultaneously committing ourselves to exploits that are well outside of ourselves. This is where the whole notion of purposive motivation or intention comes to play.

It seems obvious that leadership grounded in calling would pay homage to intention. As calling is so very explicit in its focus, intention or purposive motivation should rise as one of the salient ingredients in calling. Leadership bounded by intention is directed. It is focused. While some may fear a term like intention when cataloging distinguishing markers of leadership, as it may sound as if it promotes an autocratic, egomaniacal, narcissistic type of leadership; that is not necessarily the truth. A leader guided by intention has viewed both the organization's internal and external landscape and presents a vision that takes into consideration the ways in which the institution's resources can be used to impact both venues of its focus. The mores, the events, the very culture itself that borders the institution could very well serve as the fodder for the leader's intention. Manning Marable (1998) when describing the nascent in leadership for Harold Washington and Louis Farrakhan, offers that,

> Both individuals came into public prominence at times when racial liberalism was declining and when policies designed to safeguard civil rights and economic opportunities for Blacks were being dismantled. Both preached the doctrine of self-help, relying on resources found within black communities for group development, rather than government handouts. (p. xii)

The culture in which both leaders found themselves immersed provided the motivation or the intention for their leadership.

It is particularly in times of crisis that intentional leadership matters. In fact, it is because of the issues, the crises, and the major challenges that intentional leadership will surface. Intention craves courage. And it is not the kind of courage that is traditionally ascribed to brute masculinity. Indeed, courage, where intention is concerned, dares to disregard all kinds of competing allurements for a leader's attention. It is the courage to say no to a good idea while realizing that an affirmative answer holds the possibility of moving the organization completely off course. Additionally, courage and intention enjoy a monogamous fellowship because so often the times in which we find ourselves require the courage to intentionally speak to the issues, to intentionally inspire others to embrace a vision that will, as Grace Lee Boggs (2012) says, grow the soul. It takes intention grounded in courage to lead from a commitment to engaging the adaptive challenges (Heifetz, 1999), while the technical ones complacently and proficiently play second fiddle to the leader's attention.

It takes courage to engage in the prophetic process of critical self-reflection. It takes courage to demand that the organization one leads intentionally shows itself to itself with a scope of candor and transparency. Concomitantly, courage is necessary to forecast a future for an organization that is liberated from past structures and strictures that have dominated its function. And from that divestment, valiantly moves with intention into a future that has benefitted from divorcing itself from the vestiges of past conceptual frames and psychic prisons.

Calling that embraces anchoring, a future orientation, and purposive motivation or intention becomes evident through what West calls an aggressive pessimism. These words are not antithetical but support one another. The whole notion of aggressive pessimism pushes the leader from giving up and abstaining from fighting the good fight through a kind of anger that contends with current organizational situations with an aggressive mindset to change them. It is as if the leader faces the realities of the educational system that could lead to an explainable nihilism. Instead, the aggressive pessimism requires the educational leader to clearly see everything that could breed a pessimistic response. However, the leader's calling anchors them to engage in the warfare ignoring the pessimism that could cloud their thinking.

Courage to intentionally think differently and to perceive an organization's mission and purpose through the gaze of justice is essential for anyone who embraces the call to leadership. As such, a move will involve contention and a pugilist's skill at ducking and weaving throughout the process of institutional transformation.

This prepares us to begin a more thorough examination of leadership and spirituality. We must understand that engaging our spirits in leadership is not an endorsement of futile navel-gazing. It is not applauding a propensity toward introspection without some concomitant action. Rather, our spirits will constrain leaders to deeper, more meaningful levels of discernment while simultaneously revving us up to make a difference, to exact necessary change and to move our organizations into constructive, socially just transition. This is where the notion of critical spirituality and leadership come to align.

· 3 ·

ALIGNING THE ELEMENTS OF CRITICAL AFRICAN AMERICAN SPIRITUALITY WITH THE LEADERSHIP PROJECT

For some time, the scholarly work I have done has dared to align the tenets of critical theory with those of African American spirituality. A brief autobiographical history lesson, inserted here, will help to delineate just how I came upon critical theory and then how I connected it to African American spirituality.

My experiences as a public-school administrator and the courses I took for my doctoral degree were as distinct and dissimilar as could be theoretically and experientially possible. Allow me to explain. As a public-school administrator of an elementary school in a predominantly Black neighborhood, I saw, first-hand, the class and racial differences that undergirded the bureaucratic decisions that were made in the urban school system in which I worked. I simply did not know how to name them. And naming the experiences became very, very important to me. In my mind, naming was not merely an intellectual exercise where the prize was giving these experiences an identity. Nothing so mundane. Nothing so intellectually trite and ineffectual. Naming the condition prohibited a scattering of my attention and instead pinpointed, with relative accuracy, my focus. Additionally, naming required engagement with hard-hitting truths that were affirmed through empirical data and anecdotal evidence. Naming also required me to address the role I played in maintaining the named or identified condition. For me, accurately naming provided an opportunity to do some critical strategizing to establish the future work that would retard the continuous spread of these oppressive, institutional conditions that I will now describe.

My elementary school was not one that the system showcased. I was the principal of a Pre-K through sixth-grade school of approximately 220, mostly poor African American students with a smattering of poor, white, Appalachian students mixed in. I remember vividly the condition of the old building. Metal steps with no tread, individual desks with ink wells, chipped paint on the walls and teachers who were not sought after by principals of the more preferred or favored elementary schools throughout the district, was how my school could have been identified. That is how my school could have been named. If nothing flowed in the wind to the central office, or there was no parental tumult or teacher revolution, my little school was hardly on anyone's radar. That was until I decided to exact a few housekeeping changes.

Allow me to share more explicitly what I mean. Whenever it would rain or snow, several of the children in my building would come cascading down the slippery, metal, tread-less steps in such numbers that one could think that they had synergistically planned the mass exodus from school, those stair-accidents had caused. We would send home students each time wet weather hit. So, I decided to request from the assistant superintendent for facilities, tread on the steps of my three-story, dilapidated building. While such a request may sound both reasonable and responsible, I nonetheless, was chastised for making this request without first going through some mediation process with my immediate supervisor, an administrator called an area director. I'm unaware who made my area director cognizant that the work on the steps was forthcoming. But apparently, my area director found out and called me and lambasted me for having kept them out of the loop. I must admit that the tongue-lashing I received did not even slightly impact me as the much-needed tread was being affixed to the steps and therefore the safety of my students would shortly be enhanced. While I was on a roll, I also had the entire school's supply of the early twentieth-century desks removed and replaced with more contemporary ones. Perhaps you are wondering just how this experience and the one other I am about to narrate intersect with my doctoral studies. Your patience will hopefully be worth the wait.

I was interviewed and transferred to a magnet school. Magnet schools were created to implement the desegregation order the school system was under court mandate to enforce. There was being built a brand-new building about one mile from the school where I was then principal and that would be the school for which I would be named the new principal. Allow me to do a bit of deconstructing on this naming incident. This instance of naming was a bit convoluted and contradictory. My having been named the principal of my first school came with a host of bureaucratic restrictions. Being named principal was accompanied by a demand that protocol over my students' welfare was the preferred way for me to operate. However, being named to this magnet school unearthed for me a host of contradictions. This school, in its former life, was a historic landmark in the African American community. It was the educational reference point for many, many Black citizens. At one point in the city's history, it was one of only very few schools Black children could attend. Its history and notoriety, among African Americans in my city, were tantamount to infamy.

I was responsible for moving the school from its historic landmark to the new building situated right next to it. This meant watching the old building being torn down after moving into the new one. That move was fraught with all kinds of community opposition and legitimate community suspicion. However, the move was successfully implemented. Now, the catch with this magnet school was that because of the court order the school had to attract white children. For so many of these alternative schools, as they were once called, had attracted Black students to their facilities. There seemed to be this implacable point of view that for Black parents having their children sitting with white children held an attraction that simply did not exist in an all-Black school. Exploring this more deeply and naming the truth about this phenomenon, white schools had better-supplied facilities, had more enriching experiences to broaden students' academic investments and were assigned more well-qualified teachers. So, for Black parents to see their children being in white schools as an improvement for their education was not an unfounded perspective. In very real ways, since the truth must be told, Black families made desegregation work in our city. But my school had the mandate to attract white students. And it was in the bureaucratic machinations that accompanied that mandate, that I more pointedly saw the racial and class disparities that were pervasive in the system. I still yet was unable to name specifically what I was experiencing.

One day as I was completing some mundane paperwork, the superintendent arrived at my office. This was an exceptionally irregular event. As generally, if the superintendent had something significant to tell you, you were summoned to his downtown office. But that day he sojourned to my inner-city school office and sat down to inform me that he was the only person I needed to consult about anything I desired for my school. Whatever I wanted he would ensure that I got it. It was imperative, for the sake of complying with the court order, the superintendent affirmed, that my school would aggressively attract white students. So, there would be no middle arbitrators with whom I would have to deal. Whatever I wanted I could have. The teachers I hand-selected, I could have. The materials I wanted including the curriculum I desired to use in my school, I could have. Just attract white families to my school.

It is a matter of great significance that I reiterate that my new school was, at most, a mile away from my former school, residing in the very same neighborhood. The same social and economic dynamics were pervasive in the neighborhood where both schools were now located. So here is where my doctoral studies enter this drama.

Many of the classes I took in my doctoral program emphasized techno-rational ways of viewing educational leadership. There was no mention of critical theory or more progressive ways to consider the work of educational leaders. There were no probing questions that incisively interrogated the status quo conditions of schools and their leadership. Virtually none of the scholars that I read, while pursuing the doctorate, ever disrupted and offered a deconstructive critique of the hegemony that characterized the educational process. So, there was no vehicle through which to name the experiences I had engaged. There was within me, however, an unshakeable understanding that the ways my two schools were treated, certainly manifested a deep dichotomy, in the least. That dichotomy, I might add, was irresolvable. It additionally, highlighted the stark differences that became manifested based upon my having learned the whole notion of interest convergence from critical race theory. That is, the measures that looked like desegregation, that could be engaged to bring about educational equity, actually served the overarching need for the school system not to have to face sanctions for non-compliance with the deseg. court order. I must quickly assert that interest convergence was not a concept I had learned during my doctoral studies. I only learned of this tenet of critical race theory when I became a professor of educational leadership.

Within my very soul, I knew that I had lived within a significant dialectic but did not have the language to name it and my doctoral program gave me no assistance in doing so. Once I became a professor, after leaving the public-school system, two of my colleagues were Henry Giroux and Peter McLaren. These two scholars aligned the tenets of critical theory with education in exceptionally profound and impactful ways. My university office, being situated between the two of them, allowed the ideas of critical theory to seep through my office walls and phenomenally influenced my thinking. And above all else, the critical theoretical language enabled me to name what I had experienced as a school administrator.

Through discussions with Peter and Henry, reading the works of several critical theorists and ultimately engaging with the phenomenally impacting work of Cornel West, I was able to name, with pinpoint accuracy, the experiences I had lived through as well as to ask even broader questions about the issues of race, class, sexual orientation and spirituality in educational leadership. It was this notion of aligning African American Spirituality with critical theory that was inspired through my reading of Cornel West's work.

I was motivated to do this rather unusual exploration through the work of Cornel West (1982), when in his book, *Prophesy Deliverance*, he deigned to uncover the potential alliance between prophetic Black Christianity and Marxism. I applaud the fact that he first offers a Marxist critique of what he refers to as the "Christian dialectic of human nature and human history and the Christian critique of the Marxist dialectic of human praxis and human history" (p. 95). West realizes that the marriage of Marxism and Christianity is not without its challenges; but he nonetheless sees the value in and indeed the overall brilliance and pragmatism of what some might call an unevenly yoked union. It is from this same dialectical perspective that I have explored critical theory and African American spirituality as the foundation for a definition of leadership. Such a definition deconstructs the hegemonic notions of this dynamic that have been historically accepted as almost sacrosanct. It is this kind of intellectual, theoretical, and even disciplinary breaching and risk-taking and also coupling that West unashamedly engages, that really has inspired me to explore the alignment between critical theory and African American spirituality. Casting caution to the wind and wondering or more accurately assertively imagining how two seemingly disparate concepts could fuse with one another, became my obsession.

May I offer early on in this chapter that my views on critical spirituality, that is the blend of African American spirituality and critical theory, as I have written about before, (2005 …) have broadened. Were one to review some of my earlier work, it would be evident that I have bounded notions of critical spirituality within four basic spaces. These four have been critical self-reflection, deconstructive interpretation, performative creativity, and deliberative action. While I still maintain the efficacy of critical self-reflection, performative creativity and deliberative action, each of which will be explained in the next chapter, I have come to realize that deconstructive interpretation, that facet of critical spirituality that dares to ask the question of just how we were socialized and burdened with familial and cultural bondages that gave rise to racist, sexist, homophobic and other marginalizing behaviors, needs to be broadened and actually deconstructed itself. So, I have looked at grounding the work of critical spirituality, that blend of African American spirituality with critical theory in ways that, in my opinion, particularly deepen its meaning and influence especially the practices of Black leaders, specifically, and all leaders, generally.

The exciting challenge for me has been to explore the ways in which these two seemingly oxymoronic notions can consummate their monogamy to produce a progeny that can ground the work of an institutional leadership in acts of justice, inclusion, and purer forms of egalitarian practice. How can African American spirituality and the tenets of the Frankfurt School join forces to create a leadership of activism and indeed revolution that will foment genuinely substantive institutional and societal change? The project to come to grips with that question must first contend with an inherent, institutional push to maintain the as is and to believe that the not yet need only be a replication or continuation of the as is. A perspectival given is that when one is pleased with the status quo, there is no need to search for a theoretical thread that questions the efficacy of racist, sexist, classist practices that are reinforced through asymmetric relations of power steeped deeply in the very fabric of the institution. When you are the beneficiary of such thinking or are privileged by such a mindset, there is very little motivation to question the preeminence of the status quo. But when you and others like you have been riddled with the bullets of anti-Black racism, white supremacy and other movements of marginalization and abject disenfranchisement, your fevered search for something new almost becomes an obsession. I offer that such a blending of critical theory, spirituality and leadership portends a leadership of societal change if indeed not actual revolutionary transition. I will begin this marriage proposal by articulating the major ideas of African American spirituality.

Allow me to argue that while some may contend that spirituality is raceless, I would argue that its value is prized particularly in the Black community perhaps more than almost any other. I would suppose that spirituality may enjoy a racelessness but the proclivity to embrace it can certainly be seen as an attribute that describes action taken especially by African American people in general and African American leaders in particular.

Allow me please to cite an example. There is no doubt that spirituality has been the driving force behind much of the Civil Rights Movement in the sixties and seventies. There was, for many of the movement's leaders, an undeniable calling that propelled them and committed them to the work. Throughout Jon Meacham's (2020) text, *His Truth Is Marching on: John Lewis and the Power of Hope*, the Pulitzer Prize-winning author clearly delineates how Lewis' spirituality, his sense of calling, his perseverance even in the face of beatings and absolute human debasement nonetheless demonstrated a thorough commitment to the work. He was not dissuaded by the threats to his life and realized that his life's purpose was to provide leadership to the movement. This sense of calling was certainly augmented through Congressman Lewis' history in the Black church. But it surpassed the normal boding or harbinger of religion.

As we continue this exploration of African American spirituality and broaden our understanding of critical spirituality and the role of African American spirituality, I propose that there are five distinct elements that define the presence and function of this ethereal facet of Black life. Those five distinct elements are the *ontological*, the *axiological*, *teleological*, the notion of *faithful ideation*, and the *I/Thou element*. All five of these factors coalesce to provide the internal motivation to lead in ways that hardly mimic the traditional technical grounding in which leadership has historically been founded. Examining these five elements moves notions of leadership from the boundaries of mundane banality into a force that ignites life, promotes soul, and beckons sentience and verve in organizations. This quintet allows for visions and missions to no longer be played in warm and soothing harmonic chord constructions but welcomes nuance and dissonance as vehicles to celebrate voice. This combination collaborates to open untapped dispositions and to see deep meaning emanate from the more substantive engagements that can result from the presence of these five elements in leadership practice. These five elements serve as the foundation for calling, as was discussed earlier and its major components, anchoring, and future orientation. Let's begin with the ontological element.

Incredibly essential in leadership that is buttressed by spirituality is the position of being. This may seem to be so elementary but being and the recognition of one's being reside in very contested spaces. And the necessary step for a leadership that matters is one's settling with this ontological imperative.

Navigating the very turbulent waters of ontology for an African American can only be successful, in my opinion, through a dependence upon one's spirit.

There is so much that mitigates against such a journey because the empirical world systemically makes it difficult for an African American to embrace one's ontology. The multiple ways Black lives are physically brutalized both now and historically, the systemic contrivances that dismiss Black lives through concretized policies, institutional and societal practices and media portrayals will cause the African American to search for affirmation of self well outside the confines of just our physical existence. For some, to embrace one's ontology may take close to a lifetime because all kinds of obstacles unabashedly block especially Black people's self-acknowledgment. It is a daily fight that requires brandishing a self-confidence and an aggression to contend with the manifold ways Black ontology is buffeted. If we define our humanness through comparison to others, we will find ourselves not only frustrated but also failing to reach the goal of accepting and proclaiming our own humanity. Additionally, we lose the battle when we see ourselves as someone else's "other." We restrict our definition of self when we measure our definition of self against that of others, especially those whose humanness is grounded in privilege and notions of supremacy. It takes a spiritual commitment to name our ontology and to supersede the already accepted and unfortunate concretized notions of what it means to be a white human, the regrettable measuring rod of all humanness.

I was taken by an example of this ontological warfare President Barak Obama (2020), in his autobiography, *A Promised Land*, clearly delineates. He captures the essence of this diurnal struggle as he describes how it was manifested in his wife, Michelle. President Obama writes,

> Michelle has managed this psychic burden all her life, largely by being meticulous about her appearance, maintaining control of herself and her environment, and preparing assiduously for everything, even as she refused to be cowed into becoming someone she wasn't. That she had emerged whole, with so much grace and dignity, just as so many Black women had succeeded in the face of so many negative messages was amazing. (p. 134)

It is this contention, the very warfare that African Americans engage every day, that must be fought successfully to lead institutions under our charge in the most efficacious way. In fact, from this serious ontological battle comes the inner fortitude to lead. In the battle to assert our humanness come the strategies to thwart the missiles that are launched to perpetually diminish our self-cognizance and security in naming our own ontology. It is in the battle that the very notion of the project emanates, and its future success can be linked to the energy and the determination we have used to comprehensively live in our own ontological truth.

Indeed, it is this assertion of one's humanness that sets the stage for significant leadership action. I believe that it is out of this ontological resolution that formidable actions can be birthed. Allow me to explain, highlighting how I have been seriously thinking about my own sense of being, my own ontology and then to demonstrate how those musings can positively impact a leadership that embraces spirituality as an integral influence of its practice.

The following is an excerpt of a keynote I delivered on a zoom call in the spring of 2020. The program was convened to promote courageous conversations on the topic of Black Lives Matter. I am inserting this in the section on ontology because it is the security in our humanness that establishes the appropriate context for leadership practice grounded in spirituality. The candor and transparency in the following words are the result of deep, deep reflection on what it means to be human and demonstrate the life-impacting conclusion I ultimately reached. This is what I said during that zoom presentation.

There is no doubt, that as an African American man, I have had to muse deliberately and to think seriously on what it means to be human. I have had to do this over and over again because acts of abject abuse, dismissal and violence have made me come to grips with having to define for myself and to reaffirm for myself that I, indeed, am human. It is a sober reflective moment when you are caused to consider the truth of your own humanness. It is a somber time of self-consciousness when I have had to consider how people have the gall to determine if I am human or not. Having to think like this puts in real focus that all the accomplishments and all the advances, all of the degrees and all of the positions you may have gained can actually be reduced to rubble when your humanity is being questioned. The disregard and disrespect for a breathing Black body signifies for me that just by inhaling and exhaling, those everyday actions, cannot possibly be indicators of one's humanity. Breathing lungs and a beating heart are not the markers to identify one as being human. One could consider that breathing and a beating heart are the fundamental exercise of life and therefore, are the essential markers for defining one as being human. However, I have discovered that the definition of being human requires more than those natural indicators. When a Black man can be shot at point blank range seven times in the back by someone who was commissioned to defend and protect him, I am left to draw the conclusion that my body and bodies that look like mine are bereft of that defense and protection but are open to be objectified and dehumanized. I am left to believe that my body and bodies that look like mine can be considered to be things, objects, commodity, chattel or property. So being human cannot be localized in the natural operations of the body.

Because of a lot of thinking, reflecting, reading, and talking with others, I further am left to conclude that my being human cannot possibly be determined by the predisposition or the opinions of others. Though my humanity is so often threatened by others' failure to see me or recognize my humanness. This is a sobering mental and emotional journey to abdicate one's own sense of being human to the whims and opinions of others. That my being human hangs on the benevolence of someone else's acceptance. It is a solemn and hard to fathom idea that in some way what others think about my humanity can regretfully mitigate my own affirmation of my humanness. And if I accept the power of others' definition of my humanity that then compels me to live with a tension between acquiescence and resistance- a tension between accepting someone's evaluation or rejecting their notions about my humanness. It is a constant tension, a daily tension- a nagging and invective tension that angers me and ignites a spirit within me to make the evaluator or the one who is determining if I am human or not to know that I am human in whatever way I can get that message across.

So, I had been compelled to make a distinction between living and being human. In my mind, living and existing share a definitional space. Though some may argue that living is more substantive, more compelling, than merely existing. And while in some ways I might adopt such a position, I find that when considering living and existing in the same ring as being human, human wins the bout, hands down. I have to come to this conclusion because I can see that living does not equate with being human.

Recently, I have been poring over texts that articulate arguments on Afropessimism and Afrofuturism or the notion of Black Utopia. Frank Wilderson (2020), in his text, *Afropessimism*, has piqued my interest and my opposition and simultaneously, my agreement with the tenets he presents in his text. Reading this text comes as I am reckoning the dissonance I am living through as a Black man watching other Black men and women being murdered through the channels and platforms of social media and watching as well as walking in protests that assert the mattering of Black lives. And Wilderson argues that my humanness actually does not exist. I bristle with his contention, but I read on to find out the antagonizing and yet affirming content of his thinking. Two-thirds of the way through his text, Wilderson offers,

> Human life is dependent on Black death for its existence and for its conceptual coherence. There is no world without Blacks, yet there are no Blacks who are in the world. The Black is indeed a sentient being, but the hobble of Humanist thought is a constitutive disavowal of Blackness as social death, a disavowal that theorizes the Black as a degraded human entity (for example, as an oppressed worker, a vanquished postcolonial subaltern or a non-Black woman suffering under the disciplinary regime of patriarchy. (pp. 228–229)

Now, allow me to interpret what Wilderson is saying here that I really agonized over. The jolting part of Wilderson's assertion is that my humanness or lack thereof is ascribed by a Black man, to the benefit of everyone who is not Black. In fact, Wilderson assigns my existence to that of a prop in white people's drama. Indeed, I only exist, according to Wilderson, so that white people have a baseline other with which to compare themselves. But even my otherness does not make me human. I'm an object, an essential, existential object for white people's humanity.

I cannot tell you emphatically enough how I have fought with Wilderson's assertions. I have contested the functionalist position into which he has positioned my black life. And yet, there is something about his stance that grievously resonates with me and decrees there is some merit, some veracity, some hard-hitting, unfortunate truth to what he writes. Painfully, Wilderson places before me the very idea that the atrocities that Black people face must be understood as abjection rather than degradation. And degradation would at least signify transition while abjection speaks permanence. This is not easy for a Black man like me who has been alive through the tail end of the Civil Rights Movement, the Black Power Movement, the lie that post-racism exists because of the election of the U.S.'s first African American president, President Barak Obama and the Black Lives Matter Movement. And in each of these contiguous epochs the fundamental truth embedded in each of them has been the primacy of the humanness of Black people. Through marches, protests, sit-ins and other acts of civil disobedience, at the center of all of these has been the primacy or the fundamental demand that other human beings see and respect the humanness of Black people.

I am still grappling with Wilderson's positions as I have reached for the text by Alex Zamalin (2019) who offers a different way of celebrating my life in his book, *Black Utopia, the History of An Idea from Black Nationalism to Afrofuturism.*

Before I attempt to use Zamalin's work to bring balance, I feel required to offer that in this very process, in the weighing and the judging between contested ideas, in the very process of ascertaining the congruent as well as the incongruent ways my own thinking deals with these ideas, can be found one of the ways by which I am choosing to define and assert my humanness. I am coining a phrase here that I am calling *conscious conscience*. Somebody may say that is a euphemistic way of expressing being woke. But for me, having the ability to weigh the efficacy of ideas that have the potential to yoke my mind and emotions with them is an example of my being human. Having a conscious conscience means that I am awakened within the depths of my inner being to weigh and evaluate what it is that enhances my being. What is it about what is presented to me that adds to my health? Having a conscious conscience allows me to ascertain the morality of speech, the morality of behaviors and that mere axiological capability speaks to my humanness.

How can I say this more plainly? The fact that I can offer moral opposition, to decry injustice, to feel the physical and symbolic instruments of supremacist machinations and to therefore resist them, to me, is a clear indication of my humanness. Having a voice and coming to realize that I have a voice is an indication of my humanness. I am affirmed simply by this act of speaking my mind that I am human. I am taken by the words that Zamalin writes when he offers,

> Laws can restrict freedom and brutalize bodies, but they cannot squash sovereign mind. Intention creates imagination which becomes articulated through speech. Verbal utterances give nascent political ideas reality to the speaker, who is no longer seized by hampering doubts of their impossibility. Awareness of one's autonomy and political freedom are analytically distinct. But the first is often a precondition for the second. (p. 27)

I have a sovereign mind and because of that possession, I can exert my humanness. I can exert my own ontology.

It was at the conclusion of this talk that I knew, without a doubt, that this book on critical spiritual leadership had to be written. And I see authoring this book as a demonstration of the aligning of my ontological sovereignty with personal agency. Allow me to explain.

Coupled with ontology is the emergence of agency. And it is agency that provides the impetus for meaningful leadership that matters. Leadership that asserts an ontological confidence has the wherewithal to withstand the multiple instances when microaggressions, actions of marginalization and dehumanization occur because the leader is sanguine about their own humanness. And as such, the leader behaves in a way that articulates just how their humanness matters. It is through this acknowledgment and assertion of one's humanity that agency becomes a vital leadership practice.

Agency is a bedrock of leadership. It is the implementation of a project that is birthed from one's self-efficacy. Agency is the result of a strong compunction to make things happen. It thrives on the teleological ingredient of the spiritual foundation of leadership. Before moving further, however, let us be clear. Project does not mean the completion of some ad hoc, one-and-done assignment. By no means. Included in the idea of project is the piloting of some meaningful work that will require the intense labor of protracted struggle to see the work come to fruition. The notion of project includes envisioning, designing, constructing, and negotiating, assessing, redesigning, reconstructing, and evaluating. Project is the creation of some new order that moves the organization from the preliminary steps of rebellion to the goal of revolution and monumental reform. So, the project becomes the product of the leader's ontological sovereignty demonstrated through agency. It becomes the construction of a new idea or way of operating birthed from the conjoined acceptance of oneself and ability. An individual motivated by agency sees a societal need and feels confident that they have the wherewithal to create a leadership project to meet that need and can inspire others to collaborate with them.

One who operates through agency understands and appreciates context. They know the circumstances within which they are called to have impact and yet agency causes them to move ahead with the agenda that they are driven to implement. Agency births strategic thinking. The kind of thinking that calculates meticulously the residuals of planned disruption. It is the kind of strategic musing that never underestimates the power of oppositional ways of seeing and handling matters. In fact, the question of "what if" remains a consistent mental stream that accompanies the envisioned plan for reform and ultimately revolution. A leader who grounds their practice in spirituality juxtaposes their own sense of self, efficacy, and vision with dissonant voices and agendas that are diametrically opposed to their proposed trajectory. Nonetheless, the call that includes anchoring, and a future orientation keeps the leader on course.

I am thinking of several African American school principals with whom I have worked who have taken auspicious positions to move the direction of their schools from academic mediocracy toward academic achievement. I watched how they battled with district bureaucracy and even some of the teachers in their buildings who were convinced of the academic and social deficits that their students lived in. Therefore, the teachers' or the central office administrators' decisions about the academic prowess or lack thereof of the students, were shrouded in their questioning the ontology or the basic humanness of these students. These principals' sense of self, along with agency propelled them, however, into the protracted struggle of convincing others to see the students in the way that they had come to see them: academically capable, creative, goal-oriented, and hungry for others to see these attributes in them and to assist them in activating them in their lives. The principals remain committed to seeing their schools become spaces for students to achieve academically, socially, and yes, even spiritually. They desire for their students to know that their humanity matters and that they too have agency that will hopefully, compel them to adopt a project for their own lives and use their gifts and talents to see that project come to pass.

We see this combination of ontology and agency in the leadership of so many grassroots leaders, many of whom have never enjoyed national prominence but who have brought about positive, radical changes in their homes, schools, and communities. Ontological sovereignty grounds agency because it causes individuals to recognize the gifts and talents they possess as well as the call to use those treasures in ways to bring about substantive changes that the embrace of their humanness allows to take place.

When more closely dissecting the principals' and other leaders' behaviors, one not only sees evidence of an ontological agency but also the motivating presence of their teleology. One of the sources of the principals' tenacity has been their commitment to what they believed to be their purpose. They perceived that their lives were destined to serve as educational leaders and that their current locations were the setting where they had been commissioned to pursue their specific projects. It is important to understand that the enactment of a leader's purpose or teleology is indeed a spiritual endeavor. In fact, it is a reckoning with understanding that out of all the options or possibilities with which one's life could be consumed, their teleological disposition has pinpointed, at least for the moment, this project, this investment of their personal and professional resources. Teleology, much like the anchoring component of calling, is a major source of the leaders' retention. It is as if, despite opposition, turbulence, and disappointments, the educational leader remains grounded in this work because it greatly satisfies their sense of purpose. They understand this work as being a pivotal point in their destiny.

Leaders who lead with their spirit see themselves as those whose lives matter and as such dare to imagine projects that will cajole others to see their own humanness and concomitantly, to envision a future state that relishes the spirit of reform, reconstitution, and revision. These leaders courageously accept the challenge to see themselves as agents of change, fulfilling an agenda that bombards the "isms" that militate against people's recognition of their own humanness. There is one word of caution, however. It is important to understand that ontology and its offspring agency may often be amoral. Undoubtedly, notions of reform, reconstitution, and revision can emanate from the malevolent thinking and heinous perspectives of hate groups such as the proud boys, QAnon and those other white supremacist groups and domestic terrorists who criminally invaded the nation's Capitol on January 6, 2021. They had agency and unabashedly did their best to permanently disrupt fundamental governmental functions. And no doubt, their attempted coup was birthed from a desire to reconstitute the U.S. government, to perpetuate a white racist agenda and to proclaim that as a matter-of-fact Black life did not matter. Indeed, their insurrectionist actions were not amoral but were immoral as they were driven by a white supremacist motivation. Signs, Confederate flags, racist rhetoric, and violence all spoke to an America that gave primacy to white privilege and supremacy and the degradation of all others who were not white.

Therefore, as I write about ontology, agency, and teleology, I am culling out the highest of moral thinking and behavior that is humanly possible. Ontology and agency require an axiological covering to make certain that the results that flow from the embracing of self with the teleological confidence to be productive, create results where equal and non-discriminatory justice is equitably meted out. Where white supremacy and its cohort in crime, white privilege, are disrupted and not allowed to serve as the coins of the realm in America's democratic experiment. Where bigotry and marginalization based on race, gender, age, class, ethnicity, ability, orientation, or religion are called out and steps are taken to rid them from the very fabric of society.

The axiological element of leadership grounded in spirituality can be a contested, a very contested space. There are several perspectives about axiology, that is the field in philosophy that studies values and ethics, that even in themselves, make this a contested territory. Because I strongly believe that an axiological foundation is essential to the work of a leader, we need to take some time to understand this area of philosophical thought more deeply.

There is what Gerald Gutek (1988), an educational philosopher, calls the idealist axiology. "In idealist axiology, values are more than mere human preferences," Gutek argues. "… they really exist and are inherent intrinsically in the structure of the universe" (p. 24). Only a lack of perspective or relationships, Gutek opines, causes people to be off track in their ethical decision-making. While I am making an argument for axiology to ground critical spiritual leadership, I am troubled by the idealist's position that the world's ethical stance can be founded upon the "... permanent aspects of a social and cultural tradition that in reality is the wisdom of the past functioning in the present" (p. 24).

I shudder at the very thought of grounding a definition of ethics and values and what can be determined to be moral behavior based upon some ephemeral notions of concretized social and cultural traditions. All kinds of miscreant behavior have emanated from such established historical traditions. So, in my mind, to rely upon formulations of morality based upon idealist predispositions that manifest themselves in social and cultural mores and behaviors leaves me wanting and longing to explore and look for another.

There is then the naturalist's take on axiology. "For the naturalists, values arise from the human being's interaction with the environment. Instincts, drives, and impulses need to be expressed rather than repressed" (p. 76), says Gutek. There is one caveat to this definition and that is that the major premise of the naturalist's definition of moral or ethical behavior receives its life from a natural, self-esteem which cannot include the exploitation of others. This idea got its roots from Rousseau's notions of *amour de soi*. This argument would not allow the advancement of the self, predicated on the oppression and suppression of others. This argument applauds the primacy of the human being/nature relationship and offers that that alignment ensures ethical and moral behavior and that the love of self has a way of radiating to others. "From the love of self comes a natural ethic that cultivates a sense of human equality and institutions based on rank and privilege could not impede nor deflect" (Gutek, 1988, p. 77). I suppose I have more confidence in the naturalist's position than the idealists. However, there is way too much leeway for there to be aberrations to the very premise of the naturalist's position. The very idea that the care for others and the insurance that their oppression is prohibited through someone else's love of self, leaves me wary if this idealist strategy can assuredly be counted on to successfully fulfill this mission.

I am looking for an axiological grounding that will not acquit persons who believe that their supremacist beliefs are moral and ethical. An axiological grounding that will not approve anti-Black racism as an ethical way to believe and to behave. The last axiological position Gutek delineates is the realist axiology. "Realists contend," Gutek offers, "that our actions and appreciations can be estimated and judged by criteria that are external to us" (p. 45). There is some notion that the universe operates in rigorous patterns that possess purpose and intention. There is a design to universal operations, and it becomes the privilege of human beings to become keenly aware of these universal givens. What accompanies this knowledge or awareness is the obligation to comply with these designs and universal intentions and codified operations. Gutek offers,

> Realists encourage us to shape our values in terms of the structures of reality. By knowing the structures of physical, natural, social, and human reality, we can frame realistic and viable alternatives. Through knowledge, we can rationally frame choices about life. (p. 45)

Huge in the realist's thinking are human potentialities that include, "self-determination, self-realization, and self-integration" (p. 45). Notions of rationality serving as the foundation for ethical decision-making assist to construct the foundation of the realist's axiological position.

Again, the dependence on the self and even the voluntary move to know and understand the designs and patterns of the universe as a source for moral and ethical decision-making leaves me with questions and concerns. I am not comfortable with assigning the foundations of moral judgments to the whims of individuals' desires to learn or to be open to investigating these universal proclivities that realists maintain to be our source of comfort and confidence in the morality that is expressed through their definition of axiology.

The classic definitions of axiology were so empty of the contents that I needed. The very thought of realizing that a sound axiological position could and should ground leadership behavior remained prominently, however in my mind. Albeit I felt unqualified to create a definition that would envelop a leadership motivated by one's spirit and moral and ethical beliefs. I felt this lack of expertise because I am not formally trained in the discipline of philosophy. But that did not dissuade me from continuing to think about and to search for a definition that would comfortably fit leadership behavior in it. I felt compelled to create a critical definition of axiology that would be well suited to dress leadership that operated within moral and ethical standards.

Isabel Wilkerson (2020), in her book, *Caste: The Origins of Our Discontents*, provided exactly the contents for a definition I was searching for. As I read the following words, they jumped off the page and my visceral response was that this was exactly what I was looking for. Wilkerson does a tremendous job in delineating the substantive differences between the two concepts race and caste. Please indulge this rather lengthy direct quote from the Wilkerson text as I strongly believe that it best situates the definition of axiology that will be most useful in this case. Wilkerson writes,

> What is the difference between racism and casteism? Because caste and race are interwoven in America, it can be hard to separate the two. Any action or institution that mocks, harms, assumes, or attaches inferiority or stereotype on the basis of the social construct of race can be considered racism. Any action or structure that seeks to limit, hold back or put someone in a defined ranking, seeks to keep someone in their place by elevating or denigrating that person on the basis of their perceived category, can be seen as casteism. (p. 70)

What this delineation of difference does is to provide a foundation to build an axiological position that serves not only to expose but to also labor to challenge thinking ensconced in racism and casteism. An ethic that decries mocking, harming, and attaching a subjugated status to a human being based on being Black is definitely an important piece in building the moral structure for spiritual leadership practice. Further, an axiology grounded in the abolition of behaviors that limit and confine one's humanness to an assigned social and cultural category and denigrate those who are not in the class with privilege and prominence can most definitely equip a leadership committed to equity and justice. So, using Wilkerson's definitions, I am offering what I am calling the activist's notion of axiology. Unlike the idealist, the naturalist, and the realist, the activist's axiological position calls the leader to demystify structures and practices that defame and dehumanize individuals based on race and social position. It requires not only the act of exposing but also the execution of critical strategies to rid the institution of those conventions, systems, and traditions that harbor racist assumptions, convictions, and judgments.

Such a disposition emanates from the actualization of one's own ontology and the residual celebration of their personal humanness. Their thoughts and dispositions are comfortably embedded in an undeniable quest for all people to walk in the uncompromised jubilation of the auto-cognizance of their own humanness and the recognition of their humanness from others. The activist axiology is perhaps closely related to the naturalist position. However, it is birthed from a consciousness of self specifically germane to one's own ontology and an unflappable commitment to others enjoying the same understanding.

The fourth component of critical spirituality is faithful ideation. Faithful ideation is an essential piece to the whole notion of Black spirituality. Allow me to quickly add that faithful ideation encompasses more than the creation and articulation of a vision. No doubt, a vision may be produced in this process but the whole idea of seeing a future, of envisioning a future for the educational site is built upon the faith one has in the inevitability that a future state will be coming into existence. This concept of faithful ideation includes a faith in and a faith to see the future come to pass. It is an imagination that sees beyond the exigencies of the present and views the future through eyes of faith or very strong belief that know that bringing into existence what does not already exist is the stuff that motivates action to make the future happen. It argues for what might be called the manifestation of acts, behaviors, and conditions to become manifested because the element of faith wills and works for these future conditions to come to pass.

Then there is the last component of this extended notion of critical spirituality, the notion of I/Thou comes into play. Albeit, what a liberating feeling to know that your humanity has efficacy. What a celebration and triumph to embrace the fact that your life can very well be the vaccine to seek the reduction of racism, classism, homophobia, sexism, ageism, and ability bigotry; that this has become your teleological imperative, the very purpose for your professional life.

Let us now explore this component that I am including in African American spirituality, known as I and Thou. For many, the very phrase I and thou undoubtedly has the potential to cause one to become suspicious. As this biblically sounding idiom may suggest a righteousness that academics may find off-putting. But it is this very notion, explicated by Martin Buber, (1970) that I honestly believe assists to ground the axiological or the ethical nature of African American spirituality. Before delving into the nature of this philosophical construct, I will simply request that you placate the sometimes obtuse, philosophical language Buber uses to describe this human dynamic and soak the meaning from the language to grasp the value of the dyads he has created.

Buber, this often -called Zionist philosopher, compels us to juxtapose the essence of two different kinds of relationships. He calls the relationships *basic words*. The one he terms I-It and the other I-thou. Both are how Buber argues we human beings, "establish a mode of existence" (p. 53). He offers that the I-it mode of existence, "can never be spoken with one's entire being" (p. 54). There is a distance and even a captivating restriction on the self when engaging with objects, with the it of the universe. There is an absence, an incompleteness that characterizes the I in the I-it engagement. The person does not emit a level of emotional integration with the object, with the it. It is almost as if because there is no match of life with life in this basic word, that a shortchanging of one's humanness can be permitted and indeed granted even if not expected since reciprocity of any kind of human exchange with the It is impossible to happen.

But it is the I-Thou exchange that Buber argues requires one's whole being. This is because when one says You, one has relinquished the absence of human reciprocity and instead has entered relation. This, therefore, requires a greater commitment or investment of the I and ignites language in the relation. There is, indeed, communication between the I and You that simply does not exist and indeed, is not even required, in the I-It dyad. It is within the I-You that we may also find the third sphere of the world of relations which Buber calls spiritual beings. There is no distinct language or communication present here in this sphere. However, this is the ethereal space where creating, thinking, and acting take place and language or speaking is not essential.

It is in these second and third spheres where the sovereignty of Black ontology gains even more momentum. Because the I-You demands the investment of one's whole humanness for language and communication to be manifested, it is therefore within that communication where needs, aspirations, and predispositions can also be expressed. Issues, challenges, and alternative world views and perspectives can be offered through the instrument of language emanating from the whole I. And it is through that space that welcomes the whole being where the language of resistance and disruption of established order or hegemony can be communicated. Through such language delineation, creativity, thinking and acting may coalesce around an agenda of reform that embraces the You; that hears the You and welcomes the insights and predilections of the You.

There is respect for the You. The words and the disposition of the You have value and deserve the audience of the whole I. It is because of this affection for the You, that the I mounts a charge against all perceptions and acts aimed at minimizing the humanity of the You. Therefore, projects that militate against disenfranchisement of the You become the targets of the woke I. This has certainly been evident in those Black men and women's lives who have led the Civil Rights, Black Power and the Black Lives Matter movements and all others that were birthed from a commitment to see the You set free from the hostilities of racial bondage. To see the You realize their own humanness and to therefore ignite their own crusade for self-liberation, undergirded much of the work of all these liberatory movements. We would be remiss were we to limit notions of spirituality, that are so crucial to this

I-You dyad, to simply strategies for self-cognizance and self-expression alone. The spiritually influenced work for the I to recognize the value and essence of the other, the You, undoubtedly served as a powerful force that leaders used to bring about positive changes in society.

· 4 ·

CRITICAL REFLECTION AND THE EDUCATIONAL LEADER'S UNFINISHEDNESS

The purpose of this chapter is to articulate more clearly what have been the original components of what I have called critical spirituality. However, I come to this task replete with questions about how my former notions of critical spirituality and leadership may be applied to the current context of a lingering residue of cancerous Trumpism, anti-Black racism, overt seditions, an international pandemic, and my own questions about the veracity and sustainability of the American notions of democracy. It is within that kind of interrogative consciousness that I will unearth, beginning with critical self-reflection, the major ingredients of what I have termed critical spirituality. The other original ingredients include deconstructive interpretation, performative creativity, and transformative action.

Throughout this chapter, you will notice the prominence of the need for a leader's confession, admission, and witnessing as practices that must be used for critical self-reflection to work. While one may correctly believe that something significant is birthed from this process of self-reflection, it is the presence of the transparent confession, admission and witnessing that initiate the practice of critical self-reflection. Some who are reading this text may be unfamiliar with the very idea of witnessing removed from the courtroom venue. So, allow me to explain.

From my cultural space, witnessing has been a prodigious exercise in Black religious practice. It is a way, when people are gathered in a church setting, to pronounce how one has overcome situations and obstacles that had at one time seemed to be insurmountable. Witnessing is an announcement to others who can most definitely empathize, that you have overcome being held hostage, you have overcome issues and you have overcome challenges that at one time had overwhelmed you. Witnessing or testifying, as it is often called, results from the conclusion of an inner struggle between the desire to remain private about your issue and the need to let everyone know that you have overcome. The witnesses in my church, when growing up, would contextualize their imminent narrative through the words of a song that admitted, "I said I wasn't going to testify but I just couldn't keep it to myself, what the Lord has done for me." Concomitantly, these circumstances positioned and characterized you while shrouding you with their version of reality. But the very act of witnessing was an exuberant verbal demonstration of freedom. The act of witnessing was a joyous articulation of how one has come through and gotten over those monumental burdens that had bound them and held them fast. It was giving testimony to the grace that had been extended and expended to remove one from a place that appeared to have the potential to destroy you. One testifies to being set free from these onerous challenges and temporal realities to others who have had very similar experiences and who may not have already been relieved from their own hardships and millstones. But through your witness, through your testimony, they were given hope that while for them it was Friday, they nonetheless remained vigilant in their hope for relief resting on the fact that Sunday soon was coming.

Without this initial work of confessing, admitting, and witnessing, self-reflection does not happen. It is the embracing of the fact that a leader is not alone that is essential to the self-reflection journey. The leader's thinking impacts the environment, and the environment influences the leader's thinking. That fundamental level of exogamous consciousness is the essential groundwork for self-reflection to commence. Leaders must witness their deep connection to their context which includes their understanding of their own sense of the external fellowship with what is extraneous to them that must be forged to produce authentic educational leadership self-reflection. For the leader who is embarking on the critical self-reflection journey, their testimony is grounded in the illuminating fact that some experience has jarred their complacency. Some experience has disrupted their accepted ways of seeing the world. Their witness becomes the self-disclosure that some ways of perceiving reality that had shut them off from seeing things differently have been troubled and are now requiring serious investigation, critical investigation. To admit this, for a leader, is not a simple task. It may be more difficult to live through the internal witnessing to oneself than testifying your disrupted narrative to others.

Allow me to provide a contemporary example of the kind of testifying and witnessing a leader may engage. The educational leader may have always believed that voting is a foundation for the functioning of a democracy. But, with the onslaught of at least 40 states in the United States creating legislation to suppress the franchise right of all American citizens, the leader's testimony may question just why these acts of suppression and downright oppression are taking place. What do these actions really mean for the status and future of democracy and what they have come to personally grapple with because of the maddening presence of these marginalizing events? An educational leader who is exposed to such a reality as voter suppression can testify that they have never considered the many nuances of voter fraud this fraudulent legislation portends to eradicate. Or the leader can testify that they need more information, more data to establish their own position on this egregious matter.

Additionally, the instances of murderous actions by those who supposedly have been commissioned to serve and to protect, must be more external circumstances that demand an educational leader's reflection. If indeed the institution of education is a normalizing and socializing force in society, then surely, educational leaders are compelled to engage in reflective hours about the deaths of Aaron Toledo, a thirteen-year-old in Chicago and Duante Wright in Brooklyn Center, Minnesota as additional examples of how that protect and serve mantra has been dastardly bastardized at the hands of supposed officers of peace.

With that said, let us deepen our discussion on the essential, external ingredients that play the major role in the endeavor of self-reflection. I do not apologize for this forthcoming deliberate alignment of critical self-reflection with the manifold realities within which such pensive and contemplative ruminating must take place. One cannot lead and have their leadership influenced by their personal reflections if the very nature of the cultural, social, and political landscape, one is in, does not serve as pivotal fodder for such critical contemplation. It, most assuredly is, a facile exercise to attempt to engage in critical self-reflection sans a rendezvous with context. However, such an effort minimizes the substance of the reflection and leaves the leader myopic in vision and clueless in the essential understanding of the forces that are perpetually and progressively infiltrating the educative process. I propose, therefore that there are two unavoidable stages that comprise the work of critical self-reflection. These stages include awareness and analysis.

Education's landscape includes rugged terrain replete with boulders that demand strategic and incisive excavation. Further, the educational process comes with twists and turns that make the labyrinthine course difficult, at best, to navigate. Educational leadership has never enjoyed a flawless path to traverse. It has never been blessed to take place in a frictionless, pristine environment. While that is the absolute truth, it seems that in these prescient moments the menacing potholes, raised surfaces and unforgiving fissures and crevices in leadership's path are demanding educational leaders' undivided attention. The very presence of what Eddie Glaude (2021) has called the cold civil war that we are right now experiencing in the United States, is just one example of the troubled environment that coalesces with a panoply of other events that are requiring an educational leader to focus attention on the demands that each of them presents.

Leadership, though some may offer a differing opinion, demands self-reflection. Contrarian thinking may propose that self-reflection is one of those navel-gazing exploits that births egomaniacal or even narcissistic behavior. However, critical self-reflection purports to motivate a leader to make substantive changes that will not only impact their own thinking and comportment but will also positively impact the lives of those they lead. Educational leadership that dares to question one's behaviors and the nascent of those behaviors is the kind of leadership that can have enormous impact on the persons within the institution one leads.

As I am writing this chapter, I am experiencing a genuine sense of justification to begin this discourse on critical spirituality with the element of critical self-reflection. I feel abundantly justified to do this because I am spending an inordinate amount of time, in this season, thinking and mulling repeatedly the elements of the current U.S. environment within which educational leadership is grounded. The topography that defines schools is replete with hard-hitting exigencies that demand thoughtful attention. Further, and from a more utilitarian perspective, I strongly believe that there are personal emoluments and a host of respective remunerations that can possibly be gleaned from such a reflective process.

I would contend that leadership grounded in critical self-reflection demands one to be open and to become aware of the territory within which educational leadership finds itself. Such an openness rests upon a leader having come to grips with what Paulo Freire (1970) calls their own unfinishedness. It is indeed our acceptance of our unfinishedness that gives us access to new learning. It is our admission that we are unfinished that motivates us to have what Freire calls an epistemological curiosity that inculcates our passion to seek more understanding; to realize that we don't know all that can possibly be known and that we enhance and broaden our own lives through a crucial confession that we need to know more. There is no doubt that embracing one's unfinishedness requires a humbling concession that in some ways we are deficient in our understanding. In some ways, we are incomplete in our comprehension. In some ways, we are seriously lacking in our grasp or command of all the stimuli that bombard what happens in, around and to educational institutions. To come to that point requires a disturbance of our complacency. This demands a disruption of our status quo as well as a dethroning often of those sacred cows, those golden calves, and idols we have grown to honor and come to use in the creation of our sacred senses, judgments, and impressions.

I have been a leader in Pre-K-12 and higher education for over 30 years. However, it has been within this season that the imperative to seriously admit my unfinishedness has overwhelmed my consciousness. It is not that at previous times I believed my leadership to be impervious to context. But it is now that the confluence of so many factors has motivated me to contend with where I am lacking. Since confession is good for the soul or so I have been told, I must admit that having the manifold experiences I have had as a leader don't readily and comfortably catapult me into the unfinishedness space. I would like to believe that I have learned poignant lessons and have made monumental decisions grounded in what I already know. However, there is a freedom to be able to admit that even what I have learned, and taught others cannot comprise all there is to learn and share where educational leadership is concerned. Coming to grips with the significant understanding that we must become aware of what we have been blind to or what has been lurking in between the lines of reality is a phenomenal way to initiate the stage of critical self-reflection. Allow me to share a recent incident that epitomized my state of unfinishedness.

My admission of my unfinishedness began when a doctoral candidate on whose dissertation committee I sat, opened my eyes to the two notions of Afropessimism and Afrofuturism. Earlier, I imparted the impact that Frank Wilderson's treatise on Afropessimism and Alex Zamalin's work on Afrofuturism had on me. They both opened me to unanswered questions as well as to the stalwart positions that have birthed my dispositions and practices over the years. Both prompted me to take some retrospective inquiries as well as prospective explorations as to where leadership from a Black man could effectively stand. One of the effects of embracing an epistemological curiosity founded in one's unfinishedness, is the non-judgmental opportunity to ask questions out of absolute, unabashed ignorance. No doubt, such an admission may cause, especially a leader, to experience some mental malaise and a great deal of distress. If that indeed is the case, Adam Grant (2021), author of *Think Again*, offers a poignant pronouncement to the reluctant receiver of a new way of seeing things. He writes,

> Every time we encounter new information, we have a choice. We can attach our opinions to our identities and stand our ground in the stubbornness of preaching and prosecuting. Or we can operate more like scientists, defining ourselves as people committed to the pursuit of truth-even if it means proving our own views wrong. (p. 76)

So, I took the plunge and cast caution to the wind and said openly that my graduate student had opened a new world of inquiry for me. Admitting to my doctoral student and the other faculty on the committee that I followed the student's lead with my own inquiries, research, and exploration, was liberating and, self-efficacious. Embracing the Freirean notion of unfinishedness is a fortuitous step toward getting over yourself to enable the creation of a new, more self-aware one.

I cannot take lightly and therefore am unable to give you permission to do likewise, the absolute soul searching this experience with unfinishedness and becoming aware had for me. This experience absolutely invaded the core of my ontology. However, it was not an intrusion that brought abuse with it. Unless the deconstruction of long-held propositions and explanations can be considered abusive. What happened and what ought to be the outcome of the awareness stage of critical self-reflection, was my witness to the actual complexity of my own belief system. What became exceptionally obvious, through this salient moment, were the multiple ways in which my Black life had been shaped and how I had bought into some lies about myself and others who looked like me. My owning these lies, in turn, sustained the monolithic stereotypes those who were not Black had created for me. In fact, this time caused me to question whom I was attempting to convince of my self-worth, white people, or myself? The troubling question was who had become the target of my testimony sonorously proclaiming my value, me, or white people? I began to interrogate my leadership behavior and attempted to align my thinking with the awareness that in some ways, I was always attempting to convince white people that I had the wherewithal to lead them. I had the credentials, the education, the experience to be an educational leader and not just an educational leader but one of exceptional excellence, exceptional quality, heading for exceptional results. It was this drive for the exceptional that added to my consternation about the real focus of my attention. The author of *Caste*, Isabel Wilkerson (2020), affirmed what could possibly have been my motivation for seeking the leadership roles in education as I did. She offers,

> One cannot live in a caste system, breathe its air, without absorbing the message of caste supremacy. The subordinated castes are trained to admire, worship, fear, love, covet, and want to be like those at the center of society, at the top of the hierarchy. (p. 289)

Within me, is the very strong hope that my desire to be an educational leader has not been reduced to following patterns of mimicry that have been indelibly imprinted in my psyche by the dominance of the caste system in the United States. However, admittedly, it is difficult to unravel my thinking now from the truths Wilkerson has unearthed in her powerful text.

Eddie Glaude provided me with some much-needed respite as I was trying to come to grips with this internal challenge. He writes,

> Our task is not to retreat into the illusions of an easy identity politics either. Talk of identity politics often runs aground because we find comfort and safety in the appeal to unique experiences that are essentially our own and bind us to others *like us* (italics the author's). Instead of seeing that politics as one way to make claims about unjust practices ... and imagining solidarity and identity as growing out of the fight against those practices, we reach for something deeper, something that exists apart from history and prior to experience, that connects us to one another. (p. 113)

He follows then by saying,

> What matters-is that categories can shut us off from the complexity of the world and the complexity within ourselves. There is nothing simple or obvious about it. Embracing one's identity does not settle the matter at hand; it is the result of a life lived fully, not one with our heads stuck in the sand searching for that essential grain. (p. 114)

Glaude helped me to break open the complexity of the world and the complexity within me and to engage, sometimes painfully, with the residuals from such unearthing. Contemplating the role of categories, the confining responsibility of categories, the psychic prisons categories foment has assisted me to at least posit that maybe, just maybe my pursuit of leadership positions emanated from a more altruistic space than the one Wilkerson's caste treatise provides. In this way, I received much-needed support from Glaude's words.

I also discovered that this was not a one-and-done exercise. But juxtaposing the world's complexity with my own, caused me to raise questions that defied simplistic responses. As I raised one set of questions, another set surfaced with as much intensity and pressing upon me to get answered. Here were just a few of the questions that laboring with multiple complexities birthed.

- How has my quest for leadership come from a compunction to prove white people wrong about me and others who look like me?
- Why does my humanity depend upon another's confirmation and acceptance?
- Why should I be consumed with what white people think?
- Is my sense of self or even the construction of my sense of self enhanced through achieving yet another leadership position?
- How much of the institutional accomplishments accrued under my leadership were achieved for the good of the institution as opposed to them being the testimony to my value and the clear indication that I broke the stereotypical mold created for Black men?
- How did I get this way?
- How has this Black/white dialectic consumed such mental space over my lifetime, and
- How and why have I become sanguine with its presence?
- Why, until right now, have I not permitted to enter this discourse my position on the Me-Too Movement, the deconstruction of heteronormativity, and the anguish LGBTQ human beings diurnally face?

These are just a few of the inquiries that have surfaced through this archeological dig of my state of becoming aware. It is not the stuff of status quo development for an educational leader but indeed it ought to be.

Time for critical self-reflection is a must. Taking the time to be deliberate about self-reflection demonstrates one's seriousness about this endeavor. I began both an historical as well as a prevailing look at context. I consumed works by James Cone, Derrick Bell, C. Eric Lincoln, Howard Thurman, and Cornel West for some historical grounding. Simultaneously, I devoured books by Michael Eric Dyson, Alicia Garza, Eddie Glaude, Jon Meacham, Barak Obama, Mychal Denzel Smith, and Isabel Wilkerson to help explain what has become the "as is" of this cultural, social, and political context. This litany of critical authors freed me to confess the absence of some data and understandings that I have come to realize were crucial to assist me in positioning just what I was living through and angrily observing on all the news shows that kept me in rapt attention for most of 2020. It has been the reading of these multiple texts that has grounded my reflections.

A leader who endorses spirituality as one of the essential ingredients for their practice will engage in critical self-reflection through what is called the sacred self. These texts compelled me to listen to the perceptions emanating once again from my sacred self. In an earlier journal article, I wrote a few years ago, I defined the sacred self as the core of the individual that "celebrates an African heritage, applauds the cultural rites of Blackness, and contends against marginalizing descriptions, images, and definitions of Black life" (2005, p. 657). The sacred self has observed and carefully deliberated on the circumstances, challenges, and realities of the external world. What happens, however, is that with that observation, comes the ignition of a sense of ingestion or consumption of the facts of the observations. The nuances of what is observed become food for reflection. What underlies that which is observed becomes the motivation for further investigation. One does not divorce oneself or abscond from the realities of the context but instead ingests with a mind to critically analyze the exigencies of the truths they face in the current conditions.

It is the sacred self that is the unvarnished self. It is the self, bereft of pretense and pedigree. It is the self that welcomes a deeper understanding of its nature while positioning itself in history as well as the contemporary setting. The sacred self is so named because it eschews the hiding nature of masquerading, posturing, and fabricating oneself. The sacred self may not be, at times, the most socially accommodating because it is not good with evasion and dissimulation. But it is the sacred self that must be seated at the table of awareness when the principal meal of critical self-reflection is being served.

An educational leader who disregards the many physical and emotional atrocities caused by the COVID pandemic and who believes that the protests over police killing innocent, unarmed African American citizens, and the declaration, once again, that Black Lives Matter, have no bearing on their leadership practice or those who choose to ignore or minimize the grotesque affront to the American, democratic experiment on January 6, 2021, not only are disconnected from their sacred self, but also are actually operating in a self-induced blindness that will definitely negatively impact how they will lead. These are only a few of the contextual influences with which "woke" leaders must contend. And it is as the critical sacred self- examines the ins and outs of these issues that will lead to a leadership of substance and efficacy.

The sacred self battles to sustain its ontological sovereignty and contends against the onslaught of a nihilism that could easily take place simply from engaging with the realities of one's external landscape. It is from this ontological position, as well as the activist's axiology that the sacred self engages in the lucrative work of critical self-reflection.

The notion of self-reflection does not come without context. Reflection can only occur as the leader becomes keenly aware of the significant circumstances and substantive influences that can have impact on their leadership practices. The awareness stage of critical self-reflection requires the leader to adopt a "woke" disposition. The leader may come to this awareness space willingly, kicking and screaming or prodded by some external motivation. Awareness comes, however, through the confession of the leader's unfinishedness which then opens them to see more fully how societal events may impact their own dispositions that inevitably influence how they lead.

It is rare that one ventures on the critical self-reflection journey voluntarily. Usually, there is some instigation from some reading that opens the leader to new ideas or some conversation that disrupts the leader's traditional ways of perceiving the world or some event that shakes the foundation of the leader's thinking. What I have found over my years of teaching, is that graduate school can be that source of dispositional agitation. The readings, discussions and writing assignments that so often compile to create the graduate school culture can cause the leader to be compelled to engage with philosophies, counter-narratives, and ways of seeing the world that place them in a dialectical tension that is at once extremely uncomfortable and simultaneously a phenomenal source for personal growth and evolution.

The second component of critical self-reflection is analysis. This is where the leader works, as best they can, to separate what has become within their line of focus into its constituent elements. Analysis requires the leader to employ some investigative skills to examine just exactly more carefully what it really is that they have become aware. They are compelled to ask questions that carry them from what is the obvious to the murky waters of drawing inferences and requiring more nuanced responses to the question, what really is this.

Analysis ruptures the leader's ways of perceiving the world and acridly assesses the lenses through which the leader views what is going on around them. The analysis phase of critical self-reflection frees the leader to ask what is really happening and a more poignant inquiry, just why is this happening? I strongly believe that the why question deepens the battle and causes the leader to have to examine the very tools, mechanisms, and strategies more carefully they are using to observe and to interpret the data that are before them. Their theoretical frameworks, the ways in which they have been socialized, their belief systems, their own ontology and even their teleological and axiological positions all must undergo interrogation for the leader to admit that those have been the crutches upon which they have leaned while making slow but steady progress through this peripatetic journey.

Instrumental in this analysis work is one's penchant for skepticism. There are some who would argue that skepticism tends to obfuscate the road to progress. Skepticism, to some, forces the leader to remain unscathed by new data or ways of thinking that may have previously been tagged as being anathema to them. However, during the analysis phase of critical self-reflection, skepticism is essential. When the leader is engaged in the probative engagements of analysis, skepticism helps the leader to determine as Guy P. Harrison (2013), in his book, *Think: Why You Should Question Everything*, "what is probably real from what is probably not real" (p. 26). But skepticism does more, it is actually,

> … thinking and withholding belief until enough evidence has been presented. It also means keeping an open mind and being ready and able to change your mind when new and better evidence demands it. (p. 26)

It sounds exceptionally straightforward to embrace the benefits of skepticism when analyzing data. But to question what it is that you see and to critically interrogate what you have experienced while simultaneously questioning the lens that supports your sight or the predispositions and belief systems that are the hermeneutic used to interpret what you have experienced, can be an unsettling proposition. You are not only deconstructing the data but also the processes you are using that are militating against your deconstruction. Those processes you have been taught often by those you revere. And doing so dismantles the platforms upon which you have placed mentors, teachers and parents or significant others who have been instrumental in the formation of your dispositional stances.

It is impossible or at least impractical to underestimate the disruptive action of assessment. The process demands a very incisive interrogation of the leader's mindset and belief system. The goal is to trouble any thinking that promotes supremacist and elitist predispositions. It requires a very poignant examination of oneself with an acrid gaze on the other. Assessment brings into greater relief the I/Thou dyad and forces the leader to come to grips with themselves and the multiple others who exist outside of themselves. Because of this problematizing of the self, the assessment phase of self-reflection could very well include what Isabel Wilkerson (2020) calls radical empathy. What a phenomenal internal move this notion of radical empathy creates. Wilkerson defines this concept in this way,

> Radical empathy, on the other hand, means putting in the work to educate oneself and to listen with a humble heart to understand another's experience from their perspective, not as we imagine we would feel. Radical empathy is not about you and what you think you would do in a situation you have never been in and perhaps never will. It is the kindred connection from a place of deep knowing that opens your spirit to the pain of another as they perceive it. (p. 386)

Assessment is a combative ring where serious wrestling takes place. Wrestling with perspectives and their generation becomes a major focus of the assessment phase. Walter Fluker (1999) in his essay, The Politics of Conversion and the Civilization of Friday, in the edited volume, *The Courage to Hope: From Black Suffering to Human Redemption*, Quinton Horsford Dixie and Cornel West, editors, puts it this way,

> ... he must for the first time see himself through his own eyes and speak with his own voice. This requires a journey into the "cave"-that trysting place where he wrestles with the shadows, the appearances that flash against wall of his consciousness-a consciousness shaped by years of bondage to the name, the thing outside himself. It is at once recognition, defiance, and play: recognition of the twisted and contorted stare at one's self; insight into the incivility of the Cross which is a personal act of transgression and defiant speech; and linguistic play on a morality which signifies on all good Fridays. (p. 110)

The analysis must be the more difficult of the two stages of critical self-reflection. Because of the shadows and their genesis, those multifaceted things outside oneself that have unbelievable influence are all the substance of what is essential in analyzing the context and interrogating one's response to it. It is frightening and requires an internal fortitude to face one's foundations and their ghosts, the substructure of our belief systems and their demons, the root of our preferences and their specters.

May I suggest some guiding questions to direct the path of assessment? When one has taken off the blinders of myopic vision and takes into the environmental influences that are contextualizing what happens in the schoolhouse, through the awareness process, one can ask some of these possible questions:

- Given the events I am seeing, what could possibly have been the motivation for their existence?
- Whose interests are solidly being served by these events?
- Whose interests are not being served by these events?
- How do these events promote equity and equality, democracy, and justice throughout our society?
- How do these events demonstrate that the humanness, especially of marginalized citizens, is being respected and taken seriously?
- How do these events call into question my own position of the humanness of people who are not like me?
- If these actions are continuous, what possibly could be the negative residuals that could ensue?
- How do these events coincide with my own ontology?
- How do these events match with what I believe to be ethical and morally just?
- What can be taught and learned from these events about human motivation, the status of our society and our future should these events continue?
- How have my thoughts and actions perpetuated the original enactment and potential continuation of these events?
- How complicit am I in the execution of these events?

Absolutely no one can progress through critical self-reflection unscathed. There are emotional, mental, and spiritual accoutrements that result from this facet of critical spirituality. Engaging truth, deconstructing myths, and reconstructing belief systems sans hegemonically promoted dispositions, result from self-reflection. A leader who passes the reflective examination is prepared to then interrogate their professional behavior more keenly and to allow the results from reflection to serve as the substratum of the next facet of critical spirituality, performative creativity.

While I have hopefully established the groundwork for expounding upon critical self-reflection through its two ingredients, awareness, and assessment, I am compelled to admit that so often this kind of substantive ruminating cannot be accomplished alone. Most recently, in a breakfast conversation with two other leaders, as we talked about, most transparently, I might add, some of the major challenges our leadership was facing, we were drawn to a period of reflection where we became consumed with the several ways our own behaviors may have added to our challenges. We were compelled to think seriously about how our personal predilections and preferences may often cloud our judgment when assessing the value of staff members' contributions. We were pushed to consider what were "war-like" situations that required a certain type of leadership behavior as opposed to others that would not require that nature of leadership. We only got to this level of deep personal reflection through the probing questions each of us asked the other. The trusting atmosphere lent itself to transparency. The very fact that candor was critical and our motivation not only to deal with these challenges but also to understand their presence pushed more fully us to lay aside disguise and dissembling and instead to embrace truth and authenticity as the nature of our conversation.

Therefore, the results of critical self-reflection may not come simply as the accomplishment of significant prodding taking place as an isolate. Rather, the awareness and assessment processes may be heightened in their accomplishments through interactions with others. Sharing ideas gleaned from readings with others to experience an iron sharpening iron transaction, can often prove to be most effective when engaging in critical self-reflection.

Before we explore just how performative creativity fits within the critical spiritual framework, it is essential for us to take a moment to remind ourselves about the very definition of leadership. In an earlier chapter, I wrote that leadership is a complex interplay of a variety of elements. Those elements include visioning, listening, influencing, guiding, communicating, collaborating, and delegating. Leadership demands one having the skill to inspire others to bring their gifts and talents together to attain an objective or a goal and to do so in such a way as to be personally fulfilling and meaning-making for everyone involved.

You may recall that I also offered the three essential personal activities that compile to forge leadership behavior, those being critical self-reflection, tempered self-confidence, and self-awareness. Leadership is the practice of getting people to move with you toward some destination. Leadership is a peopled phenomenon as well as a spiritual endeavor. And educational leadership involves the confluence of all these practices and attributes focused on an educational setting.

The very nature of the educative process, that of illuminating and facilitating discovery, investigating for and to draw conclusions about truth as well as the juxtaposing of past assumptions with newly discovered ideas and concepts, demands the educational leader becomes adept at conjoining the facets of critical spirituality with their practices of leading educational institutions. Allow, then this brief review to sustain for us the reasons why the elements of critical spirituality and educational leadership are being joined in this text.

The next ingredient in my original definition of critical spirituality is performative creativity. The two portions of performative creativity have been intentionally conjoined. As we have docked in a rather turbulent harbor of self-reflection, it can become expedient, in our afterthoughts, to simply allow what has been unearthed in this first process not only to marinate but to regard also the results of the reflective process as ends in themselves. To some, the personal enlightenment that was gained through the consummation of one's thinking with the partners of awareness and assessment could be enough. This season of personal illumination, revelation and discovery may be the denouement for some leaders. However, if that is the tact taken, then the essential work of institutional transformation gets abandoned for personal, spiritual aggrandizement. All the internal work remains on center stage while much labor must take place in the very foundations and rafters and in the stage rigging and other parts of the theater that demand a leader's attention. Not to do so, leaves the educational institution shortchanged and held hostage to hegemonic practices that so often need to be transformed.

All this reflection must lead to some strategic action. Otherwise, the reflection is a hollow, self-serving operation that impacts the individual engaged in the reflection and absolutely no one else. Because critical spirituality is about institutional transformation, the reflection must lead to some movement, some venture that causes the organization to pivot on the pursuit of justice and egalitarian consciousness. West (1982) provides a succinct and exceptionally useful message regarding the purpose of reflection. He opines in *Prophesy Deliverance: An Afro-American Revolutionary Christianity*,

> The goal of reflection is amelioration, and its chief consequence is the transformation of existing realities. This process is guided by moral convictions and social norms, and the transformation is shaped by the interpretation and description of the prevailing communal practices. (p. 21)

It is the work of transforming existing realities that becomes the focus of this performative creativity. The leader spends quality time in creating ways for the educational institution to operate in democratic, fair, and equitable ways. Included here is the re-examination of the multiple ways exclusion, disenfranchisement, and marginalization have become deeply embedded hegemonic practices. Following the re-examination of these existing realities comes the grand opportunity to recast, to reimagine and to recreate an educational space that exacts liberation, social justice, and equal opportunity for all those who impact and are impacted by the educational institution.

If we embrace the assignment to transform existing realities then let us begin with unlocking the meaning and the intent of the first player in this duet, performative. The word performative has been defined as an expression or a statement that implies the accomplishment of some action simply by pronouncing the intended action. A performative statement can be something like the following, "I assure you," or "I pledge," "we vow," or "I swear." It is powerful to understand the significance of the utterance. The performative utterance really can often be the route to a commitment to action or a commitment to next steps. There is a level of cognition and a demonstration of the presence of a very lucrative process when a statement, an announcement, a declaration can be made because of the reflective stage in critical spirituality. While the communication from the deliberation is a very positive move. The making of the statement is only beneficial when it aligns with the spiritual work of creativity.

Speaking or writing the revelations gained from the critical self-reflection, forms the basis for the thinking that will undergird the creativity work. Performative creativity involves thinking that will move the gleaned revelations into ways to implement what has been unearthed. So, what has been declared becomes the fodder for innovative ideas designed to positively change the educational institution.

There are several theories that attempt to define creativity. The purpose here is not to disprove any of them. However, I would like to open our thinking to the notion that creativity is a spiritual venture. Creativity requires the leader to momentarily suspend the rules and the regulations that have bounded their perceptions over time. Creativity eschews the "as is" and boldly allures the leader to the "not yet." It is what has not yet been, what has not yet existed, that is the stuff of creativity. What is exceptionally intriguing about creativity is that it really is manifested through a permissive and proactive faith that frees the leader to dare to believe that what they have seen in their imagination can come to pass. Creativity encourages the leader to see what has not been tangibly available with the faith to design all that might be essential to bring their vision of transformation to pass.

For the leader, the act of creating a transformed future for the educational institution can become a community effort. Through performative creativity, the leader is encouraged to share publicly the contents of their reflective process. The leader unabashedly makes the pronouncements that resulted from their contemplation. It is upon this expression of ideas that the leader can reveal some of the creative notions they have been considering or may invite colleagues to join them in this life-changing and significantly creative work.

Earlier, I brought to our attention the prophetic role of the educational leader. Those who study or serve as educational leaders may find themselves hard-pressed to fit themselves, willingly within the prophetic imprimatur. However, as the leader pronounces the significant results from their time of reflection and appends these ruminations to creative ideas for transformation, the prophetic cloak covers the leader even if unwittingly or unintentionally so. I rely on James Darsey's (1997) words in his text, *The Prophetic Tradition and Radical Rhetoric in America*, which say that "In remolding and reformation lies the essential optimism of the prophetic judgment" (p. 27). Indeed, Darsey maintains that even the very act of purification provides what he calls promises of the resolution of crisis. In fact, Darsey opines that this prophetic work,

> ... provides an opportunity for the reassertion of the self as against the atrophy induced by profane comforts, and its vastness and incipient power rekindles a worshipful attitude toward that which is larger than the self. (p. 27)

Darsey's rekindled worshipful attitude toward that which is greater than the self leads to our discussion of the final component of critical spirituality, transformative action. All of this, the critical self-reflection including awareness and analysis, the performative creativity with its pronouncement of a new order, culminates in some form of transformative action. In other words, the result of this work is to move the educational institution into a new space. Critical spirituality assumes that the educational institution must remain in a constant state of reformation, a constant state of reconstitution, a constant state of re-imagination. It is imaginable that African American students can fill the ranks of advanced placement and advanced classes in high schools. It is imaginable that parents and community members can give voice to the vision they have for their Pre-K-12 schools. It is imaginable that poor children will not remain bereft of educational opportunities that will afford them the chance to explore, investigate, interrogate and question rather than to remain docile receptacles of factoids emptied into them by their all-knowing teachers. And all of this is built upon a kind of prophetic proposition that there is an optimal nature of the institution. There are significant steps that can be taken to move the institution to a space where democratic practices are the norm rather than the exception. These steps will unearth those policies and procedures that are sustained through the nourishment of separatist, supremacist dogma and anti-democratic rhetoric.

· 5 ·

INDICTING ANTEDILUVIAN LEADERSHIP

I propose that we now take a more critical and strategic look at what leadership in education should and could mean. Taking a more critical perspective on leadership in education will foment a more suspicious view of the fundamental thinking that currently and has traditionally grounded this field. This requires holding in abeyance any glorification of the systems that have been constructed because of this foundational definition of educational leadership. Further, endorsing a more critical perspective about educational leadership demands embracing a healthy tension between how educational leadership has been defined and how it might more strategically be defined when considering the complex contexts within which leadership in education is compelled to engage. In taking this critical and strategic look we will unravel the tightly knit chords that have produced the embroidered tapestry of leading schools. This will then allow us to examine the thinking, more carefully, behind the blending of colors and textures, the designs and formations that have over-time come to define leadership in education. Our doing so now, however, is an example of what has taken place before as more progressive scholars, in the past, examined the tenets of school leadership.

A more critical look at leadership in education began many years ago against oppositional voices that were content and stubbornly settled with considering only the technical, the pragmatic, and may I add, important, but not the more substantive elements so essential to leading schools. Educational administration scholars such as Sergiovanni and Carver, Deal and Patterson and Fullan, preached the leading of schools from a rather frictionless context. Such a context assumed that schools were uncomplicated, depoliticized spaces, abjectly objective and undisturbed by any of the social and cultural realities of their environs. Schools were deemed only to be compelled to engage with political phenomena from within their walls and never had to recognize nor contend with political exigencies outside their thresholds. William Foster (1986), in his text, *Paradigms and Promises*, was one of the first scholars in educational administration, to puncture holes in the balloons that were released to celebrate the traditional, white-washed notions of leading schools. He dared to apply the tenets of the Frankfurt School's creation, critical theory, to the theorization that had steadily grounded educational leadership. The mere fact that education, in the United States, was garbed in the vestments of capitalism, the predominance of racist-motivated policies, promoting white, cultural supremacy and the prevailing vestiges of injustice, caused Foster's readers to come to grips with a jolting juxtaposition of a menacing dialectic that needed to be resolved. Education's leadership privileged the maintenance of the hegemony that lifted white, male dominance and subjected all other perspectives to its privileged content. Foster offered a much-needed aperture to the predominant thinking that in many ways served as the motivation for other leadership scholars to raise our objections to untroubled educational leadership theories. Such scholars as Fenwick English, Khaula Murtdaha, Judy Alston, Jim Scheurich, Linda Tillman, Colleen Capper, and Kofe Lomotey, Floyd Beachum and Carlos McCray were some of the pioneers in calling for a critical, anti-white supremacist, justice lens through which to view and practice educational leadership. Ours was a scholarship that demanded educational leadership theorists deal with the multiple injustice elephants blatantly roaming the room, extrinsic to the schoolroom that had extraordinary impact on what took place within the walls of the schoolhouse. Nonetheless, the educational leadership purists did not relent in their supposition and arguments that a more conservative, techno-rational way of leading schools was far superior to the ideas being promulgated by the more progressive leadership scholars.

Allow me to conjecture some possibilities for the vociferous opposition. When one does not respect and engage the unmistakable prominence of political vicissitudes and disregards the transpositions political stances hold on the educative process, one demonstrates and operates from an unaffected simplicity. One performs in an abbreviated version of the drama that is education. When that happens, a leader in education focuses microscopic attention to the trains running on time without regard for who is and who isn't on board, whom the train passed by, the train's destination and if the train has the wherewithal to transport each passenger safely to their unique destinations.

Indeed, leading schools or educational sites, has for too long, been reduced to matters of budgets, personnel, curriculum, buildings and grounds, assessments, licenses, certificates, and a host of other mechanical obligations that result from responding to the inquiry of "what" and "how" without ever considering or even raising the question, "why." It is so much simpler and requires so little self-investment when responding to the "what "and "how" interrogatives. There are policies and procedures, manuals and codified practices that mandate the "what" and" how" responses. In fact, a leader who is focused solely on responding to these questions, once they familiarize themselves with the procedures and regulations, for them, leadership can become robotic, and they become a cyborg, in fact, while carrying out these technical proscriptions.

An aphorism I believe that adequately describes educational leadership is, the perspective a leader possesses of education cultivates the definition of their leadership. Essentially, how the leader thinks about, perceives, or considers what education is, forms the parameters within which they define educational leadership. For so long, there has been a hegemonic view of education that has limited its existence to buildings, traditional renditions of the teacher/student dialectic and accepted notions regarding its purpose. Those perceptions have birthed very limited views of the leadership that stands at the helm of what I would believe to be a mammoth ship that has steadily drifted off course. Those perceptions have privileged some of the passengers while marginalizing and in fact, failing so many others.

There is a stated destination for this ship's journey. However, even the destination is problematic and holds within it disdain for those passengers who seek some other port of disembarking. For those, historically white men, who have framed what Jarvis Givens (2021), in his brilliant text, *Fugitive Pedagogy: Carter G. Woodson and the Art of Black Teaching*, calls the American School, the destination point for education is its preparation of the students to pursue the American dream. The American dream and the American School are both fraught, however with inherent inconsistencies, lies and systemic contrivances created to extend indulgence to some and injury to others. At the core of education is the imputation of largess to the privileged and loss to those who are in any one of the antithesis categories of the accommodated and celebrated who have been relegated to traveling in stowage. Historically and what is the current case, white students in this education space are afforded approbation while Black and Brown children are viewed and treated with disrespect, disregard, and disdain. It is therefore in the myopic definition of education that this restricted version of leadership emanates.

When I consider the function of education in my own life, I am left with varnished and even gilded images from my earliest experiences with this educative phenomenon. The whole notion of formal education was founded first on the primacy of my going to school being compulsory. Someone had decided that for society's welfare, perhaps more than my own unrequited benefit, it was compulsory for me to attend school. Further, it was mandated that from a certain age until I reached a certain age, for me to breach the compulsory education requirement, was to be considered an illegal act. Were I not regularly in the building where education was carried out my parents would be found guilty of breaking the law. The law demanded my consistent attendance in a building where it was presumed education took place.

Just as significant as the law, was the place, the venue where education was operationalized. Interesting to me, is the fact that the nature or the structure or even the primary use of the venue did not really matter. Any building could be deemed the legitimate space to house the sanctioned or canonical operation of educating. Allow me to provide an example. I spent kindergarten through third grade in the classrooms housed in a wing of a large Jewish temple. I was always intrigued by the blend of harmonic and dissonant sounds of worship that could periodically waft through the halls when I dared to breach the border between the sanctuary and the classrooms. I would sometimes enjoy a modified tour of the rest of the temple on my way to the restroom. Later, in my adolescent years, I heard of what was probably taking place in the temple such as the celebration of Rosha Shana and Yom Kippur. What was intriguing, however, was that everyone could hear the music, the language that did not even closely resemble the language we spoke at home or even in our neighborhood and the chanting of who I came to learn was the cantor. But absolutely no one took the time to educate us on what was taking place in the place assigned as the spot for our education. No one sensed the presence of a teachable moment in a building that was serving as albeit, a temporary educational space. What was going on periodically in that building that I would have to assume was unfamiliar to most, if not all of us, did not strike any one of the adults as a sage opportunity to teach us about a culture with which we had no familiarity. And yet, the building was designated as an educational site. Contemplation on that whole four-year segment of my life, has motivated me to question just how education was being defined then and more inquisitively, I am compelled to ask is education clothed in the same restricted, tightly, slim-fitted apparel, today. What was then and is taught now was codified. There was, when I was a kindergarten through third-grade student and is sadly still the case, no assumption that investigation and discovery, extant from what had been the concretized curriculum, was reckoned to possibly hold any significance, worthy of some of our precocious engagement who were in the temple for education.

Let us go to an even finer grain of interpretation as we consider education and space. In my example from childhood, what must be evident is that the entire building, the entire temple had not been granted educational status, at least not for the Black children who attended rented spaces in the building. Our education was restricted to the classrooms that interrupted the flow of the corridors and in fact, became the legitimated bastions where education could legitimately take place. What I came to learn was that only those classroom spaces held for me the treasure of knowledge. These were the anointed spaces where my approved education would take place. In fact, in my formative years no other place carried the imprimatur of a sanctioned, sacred space where the educative process would take place for my life. That space limitation also severely restricted my seeing other venues as places where I could learn, especially life-lessons that were not taught in the legitimized educational spaces. Before leaving this discussion on space, there is a remarkable demarcation that also stands out to me that occurred between what was taught Monday through Friday from 9:00 to 3:30 in the temple and the lessons that were instructed on Saturday and Sunday. A completely different curriculum was offered to the Jewish children who sat in the same seats as we did only on different days. Perhaps that is yet another example of how a differentiated curriculum lives and breathes based on children's identities. Even broader than the separation of religion from the curriculum, could this difference in what was taught represent a clear example of what someone conjectures a certain group of students should learn and what others should not? Or was the curriculum on the weekends simply evidence of the broadened and augmented, expanded, and widened course of study meant for some children and not for others? And is it possible that even a modicum of exposure to the actual purpose of the religious edifice would have breached the purposes for why my

5–9-year-old colleagues and I were temporarily schooled there? I am simply positing for some consideration that the inclusion and exclusion of students to curricular expediencies, based on their identity, was evidenced in my primary grades experience.

A more critical position on defining education would have to implore the surfacing of the multitude of both formal and informal spaces, the legitimated and the unauthorized spaces where education can occur. There must be the belief that teaching, and learning can take place wherever teachable moments erupt. In this way, education adopts an almost encyclopedic landscape that legitimates the teaching/learning dynamic in whatever space it may occur. Significant to this way of unraveling the tightly knit notions of the place of education is the need to untangle the legitimacy of the person given the privilege to provide the education.

In my family, when I was growing up, the teacher was to be revered. In fact, in the minds of my parents, the teacher was almost infallible, sacrosanct, and held authority over my social and intellectual life while in that building called school. Somehow, even in unspoken expectations, in my home, the assumption was that the extensive volume of the time-honored curriculum I was to learn was to come from the adult in the front of the classroom, the teacher. Inherent in this dynamic was the assumption that I brought an empty slate to this educational experience upon which the omniscient teacher would record all that had been deemed to be the knowledge I was, at each grade level, to consume. Indeed, the curating of my intellectual personality was dependent upon the benevolence, intellectual prowess, and communicative abilities of the single adult in the room, the teacher.

I am somewhat embarrassed to admit that it was not until I was being trained to become a teacher, myself, as an undergraduate, that my concretized notions of the teacher/student phenomenon were bulldozed as I was exposed to the radical Brazilian philosopher, Paulo Freire's (1970) *Pedagogy of the Oppressed*. You must understand that as a baby boomer, I lived amid the militancy that was unabashedly displayed through the late sixties and seventies. I lived through the organic interrogation of all things incorporated. I lived through the expressions and indeed the demands for freedom and liberty from all the voices of the oppressed, marginalized and absolutely, demoralized human beings in this country. And it was within that context of what I would call essential subversion that I came to read *Pedagogy of the Oppressed*.

I came to the stark revelation of the systemic reality of Freire's notion of banking education. My eyes were opened, and I was compelled to confess that for almost all my educational experience, I had been overtaken by the instructional methods of banking education. I am unable to more accurately describe banking education than how Freire has in his seminal text. While he articulates 10 distinct behaviors that are evidenced in banking instruction, I will only name here a few of them. Freire provides this litany of what he calls attitudes and practices that mimic, only too keenly, the oppressive habits of those with power in society. Here are a few Freire outlines,

> The teacher teaches and the students are taught.
> The teacher knows everything, and the students know nothing.
> The teacher thinks and the students are thought about.
> The teacher talks and the students listen-meekly.
> The teacher disciplines and the students are disciplined.
> The teacher chooses the program content, and the students who were not consulted, adapt to it.
> The teacher chooses and enforces his choice, and the students comply. (p. 54)

These ideas not only resonated with me but also demonstrated how the process of education was a well-oiled vehicle for perpetuating the societal status quo. The existence of racism, sexism, homophobia, and other marginalizing perspectives of people who were not white and male was solidified and assured through the teaching practices of the educational process I had experienced from grade school through my junior year at the University of Pennsylvania. There were operations inherent in the educative performance to castigate progressive, counter-normative thinking that could usurp not only the system's authority but society's very foundation. And it was through these revelatory years that the impetus to enact change in education so that the machinations that propagated oppression were not merely revealed but also eradicated was, for me, firmly established. That sense of essential subversion remains a prominent building block for my commitment to revise the pervasive educational perspective and its relic notions of leadership.

Perhaps another proposed justification for this commitment to what I will now call *antediluvian school leadership* is the fact that from its inception, education was never designed to serve anyone other than white men. William Watkins (2001), in his book, *White Architects, Black Education: Ideology and Power in America 1865–1954*, provides an accurate assessment of education in the United States. He writes,

> Education has been romanticized to the extent that, like religion, it appears disconnected from the world of power, partisanship, and shaping of the social order.

> Humankind's thirst for knowledge, like the quest to understand its existence, provides the ideal terrain for this to occur. Organized education, much like organized religion, has long been influenced by the power structure, the state, and those with an ideological agenda. (p. 10)

As we explore the particularities of traditional education, it is beneficial to deconstruct and then to redefine what education should mean. Concomitant with an essential revisionist definition of education, a definition of educational leadership must evolve into a fresh existence to subvert education's hegemonic prescriptions and to endorse a new foundation of the field. Since its inception education and specifically the emphasis on literacy has been enjoined to fulfill a purpose. Learning to read was intimately tied to the exercise of citizenship, which was founded primarily on three characteristics, land ownership, being white and male. Therefore, anyone who did not fit in that tightly woven fabric of citizenship was left out of the educative process. There was no need for them to read as they were sonorously absent from the conversations on commerce or government. Now that education has evolved to a somewhat universalist prescription, it is essential to create a more accurate definition of its purpose and its leadership.

I use the term antediluvian because educational leadership has embraced antiquated notions of education's purpose and the ideological agenda Watkins writes about and the field has labored to maintain archaic forms and perceptions about the very essence of the educative practice. For so many, education in the United States has not worked. It has become a perpetuated system ruled by an agrarian calendar, diminished in its importance due to its feminized framing, and has remained complicit if indeed not instigative of the marginalization of Black, Brown, and poor people ever since its foundation. I would argue that we must transform our thinking about education, writ large and to then create a leadership that will help to bring to pass these new definitions of what education means.

Allow me to argue that education is an intellectual process where the mind is positioned to evolve and to consider through discovery, investigation, and interrogation, the complexities of truth. It is an engagement that celebrates exploration and thrives on inquisition. Education welcomes its own unfinishedness while continually seeking new ways of perceiving and positioning, new ways of constructing and construing what has already been codified as the hegemony. Education recognizes the genius of ambiguity and ambivalence and invites a comfortable ambling within these murky avenues. Nothing is ever settled in education. Challenges to accepted understanding are always desirable, always refreshing and always generating new vistas for investigation.

An antediluvian leadership believes that ideas, concepts and even ideologies that have been accepted and honored as truth should be preserved through the administrative structure. Preservation over innovation is the grounding within which an antediluvian leadership in education wallows. Policies and practices that maintain and mitigate change and challenge are pushed by leaders who are committed to reinforcing the status quo. And while there is a tinge of quixotic romanticism in this definition of education and its leadership, it is only through an overthrowing and not overhauling but an overthrowing of antediluvian leadership that education can evolve to include those who think divergently, who question epistemological certainty, and who desire to push our understanding beyond our extant knowledge. During the COVID pandemic, our understanding of technology was pushed into new frontiers. Teachers, students, and school administrators had to come to grips with a mandatory evolution of their understanding of the mechanics as well as the efficacy of the technological world. Educators who had never plunged themselves into the unfamiliar waters of technology found themselves in the precarious position to either sink or swim in order to meet the requirements of distance learning and remote instruction. Questions, insecurities, frustrations and ultimately answers became the process that most educators faced during this challenging season. The field itself had to embrace inquiry, discovery, ambiguity, and a releasing of the traditional ways of thinking about instruction to meet the mounting demands of teaching while shrouded in this global pandemic. So, the mind of education itself had to evolve, extend, and enlarge itself to remain relevant and useful.

Education is also a mechanism for enculturation. Whether we agree with this or not, schooling has been one ordained institution charged with propagating the accepted and codified positions on cultural codes, covenants, and conventions. The protocol for patriotism, social interactions and even the appropriate responses to various stimuli, find their dissemination in the compliant and exceptionally willing walls of classroom spaces. Gender roles, persons to be honored, what has been deemed to be appropriate behavior, ideas to be paid homage, as well as what should be accounted as rational are all on the enculturation agenda that schools traditionally unquestionably assume. However, the act of enculturation rests on the fact that there is no one, monolithic culture that should be propagated. The very make-up of the U.S. militates against the preaching of one culture to define life in this country.

Notions of nativism and race and class supremacy, the primacy of white male domination in all things, must not be the foundation upon which enculturation takes place. In fact, it is the crucial interrogating and ultimately dismantling of these prejudiced ideologies that must serve as essential ingredients in the enculturation process.

Enculturation is a complex process; one that must be subjected to critical analysis and disruption. This is so because inherent in hegemonic renditions of enculturation has been the celebration of white, male, heteronormative notions of culture and all others are either ignored, marginalized, or misrepresented, at best. Somehow, the act of enculturating must be disrupted to the point where the hegemonic features that have prevailed are not only critically interrogated, but they are replaced with far more extensive and inclusive components of the defined American culture. It must also be understood that schools' position in enculturation is simply one of a multitude of vehicles that play prominent roles in this endeavor. Powerful is the variety of predispositions, ideological stances, and pivotal privileged positions that coalesce to bring about the act of enculturation. Schools or educational systems represent one way to make this happen but must be open to the fact that they, so often, are limited in their scope, restricted in their view, and constrained often by the grounding of their perspectives. Schools' perspectives are so often shrouded by the vestments of state legislatures that hold prominent influence on the ways that schools may see aspects of their work including curriculum and pedagogical techniques.

There is a moral, an axiological premise that must permeate the enculturation endeavor of education. To one who basks in the undisturbed comforts of a more conventional idea of enculturation, the very notion of incorporating an axiological presence in its definition and operation may seem to be anathema. However, to consider enculturation without a moral presence leaves this very serious act of indoctrination bereft of truth and optimal usefulness.

We can see the ways in which the status quo proponents of enculturation find progressive notions such as critical race theory to be blasphemous and anti-American. It is only because of deliberate or informed ignorance that critical race theory and requiring this theoretical construct to cry, "unclean, unclean" that the truths of this framework are deemed to lose their potential influence on the culture of the American society. I use the term deliberate or informed ignorance because many of the opponents of critical race theory don't know the principles and tenets of this work and have chosen not to know the substance of this theory on purpose. This is because the people who are offering such vociferous opposition have attempted to refute the tenets of critical race theory through specious arguments grounded in white supremacist superstitions, stereotypes, and suspicions. There is even a more heinous outcome from the attack on critical race theory. That is the regulation of academic freedom, particularly in institutions of higher education as well as the refuting of the fundamental tenets of democracy. Through these, right-wing onslaughts, the fragility of America's democratic experiment is clearly exposed. The ways in which both legally and clandestinely democracy can be abridged and almost aborted have been manifested through the multiple legislations to limit franchise or voting rights and the "book burning" like machinations against critical race theory. The counter voices from traditional tropes of American history and governmental structure are steadily being silenced and the danger of adopting the single story is being completely disregarded.

In its purest form, education welcomes multiple stories. Education sees the value of perspectives vying for acceptance as truth as one of its most prized possessions. To limit contending discussions impacts the efficacy of investigation and discovery. It perverts the purity of interrogation and cognitive difference. And this perversion is taking place all over this country. School boards have mounted prodigious campaigns to unseat board members who dare to endorse critical race theory as a part of the history and social studies curriculum. Uninformed parents and other irate citizens who have embraced the erroneous information about this theoretical construct from the right-wing media, are making demands founded upon fear that what critical race theory unearths is un-American and resonates with communist leanings.

It is virtually impossible for the host of those who are protesting to even possess a modicum of understanding of the essential components of critical race theory. Its very existence emanates from a deeply scholarly, obtuse theoretical premise that many professors and doctoral students have grappled with for elucidation and greater revelation of its premise and contentions. My goal is not to insult the protesting public but to contend that if they understood the very dense notions that undergird this theory, they would see that critical race theory illuminates truths about the American society as well as commends the telling of counter-narratives that fill in the gaps as well as complete some of the incomplete details of the American story.

This is an axiological issue because leaving out the tenets of critical race theory or any other discourse that welcomes non-white, male pronouncements from the enculturation conversation forces that process to be inaccurate and breaches an ontological imperative that requires the culture to grapple with the provoking reality that Black Lives Matter. An historical account that denies the humanness of every citizen is plagued with the pox of elitism, exclusion, and abject falsehood. The pervasive fear of including a theoretical construction that focuses on the prevalence of racism is believed to strategically subvert the accepted historical underpinnings of the American culture. To give a nod to the efficacy of critical race theory would demand that the prevailing, currently preached truths of American history would suffer castigation and revision because the presence of the rest of the story brings into question the veracity of what has been accepted, preached, and taught as the authorized, canonical history of this country for countless generations. It is not just critical race theory but the inclusion of any ethnography of "othered" peoples that dares to offer a counternarrative to the prevailing American story, that promises significant threats to what has been touted as truth. Attempts to silence the LBGTQ community in the American historical conversation, minimizing or more dastardly mythologizing, to a very negative extent, the history of the Native Americans and overtly as well as covertly applauding the evils of misogyny has been the modus operandi of the American historical project. And not celebrating the concretized historical narratives of the United States is a poignant agenda item for the hegemonic educating process that is being applauded by traditionally minded educational leaders.

An antediluvian school leadership would undoubtedly honor the extant provisions of the American historical conversation and would side with those determined to maintain it while offering multiple provisos to ensure that critical race theory must not have the remotest possibility of impacting the celebrated rhetoric that currently engulfs American history. What I offer as a complete disruption of the antediluvian framing of educational leadership is one founded upon critical spirituality.

In an earlier chapter, I have outlined the major tenets of critical spirituality. Here, however, I want to more clearly articulate how subscribing to these notions that align Black spirituality and critical theory with leadership can transform leadership practice. Because Black spirituality has always breathed life into the Nubian body and spirit, that have, without ceasing, dealt with the threats of physical, emotional, and psychological annihilation under the auspices of a white-dominated exercise of a veneered-democracy, the exposition and engagement with the atrocities of racism and supremacy wherever they have reared their ugly heads has become a steadfast agenda item for a leadership steeped in critical spirituality. One has a heightened consciousness of those societal machinations deemed to be the perfect vehicles for thwarting the advancement of those who are Black, Brown, poor and "othered." It is not that leaders who have critical spirituality in their quiver of weapons to combat hegemony merely intuit the presence of these marginalizing strategies. But it is their ability to sniff the scent of marginalization, to discern the presence of partiality and prejudice and then to create efficacious strategies to combat them that becomes the overriding focus of their work. Along with discernment comes a courage to make the right things happen. It is as if the leader who leads through the critical spirituality gaze understands the powerful link between academic labor and the struggle for civil rights.

Being conscious becomes a major ingredient in the critically spiritual leader's regimen. This is a leader who is animated through a consciousness that welcomes the opportunity to lead for transformation. Those ugly displays of subjugation based upon race, gender, class, and sexual orientation become the targets for which the weapons of the academic enterprise and social justice pinpoint. Suddenly, what happens in educational sites has a deeper teleological character. Suddenly, what takes place in classrooms is recognized for having a prophetic mark on the national culture, writ large. It makes the education project one that enjoys a deeper meaning than merely being a vehicle to a career. Rather, what happens academically is laced with the taste of the bitterness of inequality and the acerbity of white supremacy. And the brackishness of these aftertastes compels the leader to ensure that education sites become the locations of resistance and subversion against these atrocities.

A leader whose theoretical frame rests in critical spirituality comes to grips with the exposure of unequal health care for Black people that has been brought to bear through the COVID pandemic. Such a leader would challenge teachers to use the pandemic as a teaching opportunity while fulfilling mandated curricular obligations. The presence of this global issue becomes the fodder for academic investigation. So many academic disciplines can be called to explain what is happening here. No doubt, economics, political science, epidemiology, mathematics, history, Africana studies, sociology, education, social work, biology, and anthropology can be tapped as resources to grapple with the continued presence of this inequality.

The political and humanitarian travesty in Afghanistan and the American role in its existence is yet another ground upon which teaching and learning opportunities exist. The near destruction of the island of Haiti, due to both natural and political disasters, also requires the investigation of students in a learning environment to grapple with these real-life challenges.

A leader with a critical spirituality foundation welcomes such investigation and sees it not merely as a matter of relevance but as the substance for intellectual as well as activist projects. What happens in this kind of atmosphere is what Freire () calls praxis. This is the blend of reflection with action. It dares to blend academic work with civil rights action and encourages the facilitation of such an atmosphere within the walls of the school. Such a leader views nothing as being untouchable and welcomes intellectual exercise to promote humanitarian solutions to pressing societal problems. School then becomes the laboratory for interrogating thorny issues through intellectual tools aimed at soliciting resolutions, creating different societal structures, and dreaming of more divergent ways to become more human with one another.

Finally, a leader who is predisposed to seeing their work through a critically spiritual lens is one who displays great courage and faith. Courage, because such leadership will be seen as contrarian to traditional notions of educational leadership. It demands courage because its foundation is based upon an alternative narrative that sees education as far more than preparing students for careers. Courage is essential for this kind of leadership because it views the work of the educational leader as one that is not only technical but as Ron Heifetz has defined, much more adaptive. There is the constant battle between sedimented ways of seeing the world and the more progressive and critical lens that proposes new and more egalitarian ways to view life in this society. This kind of leadership can be lonely. So, the leader who espouses the tenets of critical spirituality must be able to operate from a genuine knowledge of oneself and launch on an intentional journey to look for colleagues who can support even if not totally subscribing to this way of leading educational venues.

· 6 ·

THE CONCLUSION OF THE MATTER

There are hardly ever times when being a leader is easy. Of course, I am assuming that being a leader is being defined well outside of the traditional notions of leadership that historically celebrate what one might call autocratic definitions of leadership. Undoubtedly, there are monumental circumstances and monstrous challenges that face leaders in every era. However, it is during this time of a worldwide pandemic, the instability of democracies across the planet, the resurgence of supremacist ideologies and the minimizing of the very mattering of people's lives that leading, especially in educational establishments, in such a context, becomes almost untenable. Leading, particularly of educational sites, takes much more than technical techniques and management maneuvers especially during this season. There is the increased need to make what happens in schoolhouses relevant to the protean nature of the everyday. There is never a day when something monumental does not take place somewhere in the world. And the impact of those events can be felt ostensibly within the walls of the school even if not articulated openly by the students and teachers and even the administrators who are in these educational spaces.

Historically, schools have operated as though they were immune to the events that create their context. However, these contemporary times are often filled with so many quotidian, traumatic crises that it is virtually impossible to ignore their presence and indeed even less plausible to ignore their impact. It is essential for those currently serving as educational leaders, those who desire to become educational leaders and those who are preparing them, to more fully comprehend that there is more to this notion of leadership than announcing edicts and pronouncing orders that one demands to be followed. There is more to leading than implementing the newest classroom observation techniques, reviewing lesson plans, and evaluating teachers and other members of the staff. Most definitely those practices are important but even these are located within a context of purpose and premeditation. Undoubtedly, those leadership acts are grounded in some predisposition that sets the standard for what is deemed to be quality instruction, what is the act of instruction in the first place, what is its intention and can all these questions be definitively answered in this classroom observation process. Even in the issue of evaluating personnel, the greater question than if someone is doing their job is, if they are performing with a commitment to justice and equity while attending to the more mundane but essential responsibilities of the job? Do they understand the significant ways in which their performance enhances or diminishes the mattering of all the lives they touch? Are they doing their part to assist students to see their role in transforming society through their talents and gifts? Leading from a critical edge understands that the status quo is always up for disruption.

The current ways in which racism and sexism, homophobia, and xenophobia rear their ugly heads are fodder for a critical educational leadership to demonstrate its project to use the schoolhouse as a bastion for ameliorating those societal ills. This is advanced through a leadership praxis of exposure of these societal issues, deconstructing their foundation in history and cultural hegemony and offering students the opportunity to construct creative ways to bring about radical change in those social bulwarks that appear impervious to interrogation and elimination. This is exceptionally hard work for the critical educational leader. It involves the very soul and spirit of the leader that some would prefer to remain untouched or at least, respectably sheathed when performing the responsibilities of an educational leader.

School leadership that takes on a critical cast fully sees the curriculum as one influenced by events that are top of mind for students and teachers. Issues such as food deserts in certain neighborhoods, the demands by workers for more meaningful work and more substantial wages, the overwhelming impact of wrong messages regarding masks and vaccinations, gerrymandering and drawing unfair congressional districts, the threat to the American democracy should the franchise be eliminated, what does it mean to be patriotic and are demonstrations such as taking a knee at athletic contests undemocratic, can become the foundation upon which English, mathematics, science, history, music, art, theater and other disciplines' assignments can be built. Compelling students to think deeply and critically about these challenges opens both their curiosity and their creativity and portends some possible resolutions to these nagging, persistently present issues.

Leading is a matter of contending with contexts and having the courage to focus attention on the espoused purposes and projects that are the ultimate reasons the education enterprise exists. Educational leadership is not for the faint-of-heart because the demands are so compelling, so serious, solemn, and so sobering that a calling or a commissioning to do this work is what initiates as well as preserves and retains the leader in education.

Some may argue that this text on leadership is bereft of specific pragmatic methods to operationalize critical spirituality in an educational space. That indictment may be accurate and simultaneously justifiable. From its inception, however, this treatise never did portend to be a how-to manual to implement the tenets of critical spirituality in a leadership space. It was never the intention of this book to share with the reader the best practices that should be emulated in their leadership practice. Rather than articulating what to do, the more significant purpose of this text has been to discover why to do or to understand the motivation to do and the socially just reasons that undergird what to do. What is more important than providing a leadership manual is taking the opportunity to individually reflect on how critical spirituality can be useful for an educational leader. What is as important is the essential journey an educational leader takes to engage with notions of purpose, alignment to something greater than themselves and the calling to apprehend an agenda for justice and to saturate an educational setting with the residuals from such engagement. Equally as significant is the arduous task of contextualizing the academic or intellectual work of schools in the environs that surround them and coming to realize that such a setting creates the relevance of the curriculum, and the meaningful societal impact academic labor can have. So, school leadership that is grounded in critical spirituality takes at its very source the clear understanding that the academic mission of a school is not isolated from the social change imperatives that accompany that intellectual work. This means that the schoolhouse does not operate in a vacuum but is inevitably bombarded by those events, dispositions, and the complexion of the world around it. I wholeheartedly recognize that I have made this point throughout the writing of this book, perhaps to some readers, ad nauseum. However, I am convinced that for so many, educational leadership has been reduced to what happens in a site, what takes place in a structure that has been devoted to the educational process and leaving alone what happens outside its doors. It unfortunately has been reduced to reading, writing and arithmetic. In recent years, education has taken on the more targeted push to provide more students with STEM opportunities so the United States may more ably compete with other nations in science, mathematics, engineering, and technology. And unfortunately, if this mindset remains, then the genuine efficacy of the educational process is missing. The life-impacting essence of education loses its prowess when reduced to the mere instruction and learning of curricular bites disconnected from the lived realities of the students, teachers, administrators, parents, and community who participate in the educational process.

Most recently, I read the email post of a university provost lauding the number of prospective students who had applied to the university. According to the provost, the numbers were at an all-time high. While I certainly understood the motivation for the provost's celebration, I simultaneously wondered if the incoming students to that university are going to be challenged to find their purpose and calling through the academic exercises and co-curricular experiences they will have. Will they engage in an urgency to make sure that their intellectual engagements will result in the lessening of supremacist behaviors throughout society? Will the students be challenged to engage with facing their own role in perpetuating certain racist and sexist practices? Will the students then find themselves motivated to do something to rid society from such behavior? I know that this is asking a lot of the educational enterprise. But I strongly believe that at the very founding of schooling in this country was the challenge to use it as a tool for the procreation of democratic practice. At its core was the establishment of a culture that not only bristled against authoritarian rule but also rigorously fought physically to see it never become the norm for the new American colonies. Promoting democracy has been at the very root of the educational enterprise. How desperately that motivation needs to return.

Allow me to share with you another heart-wrenching experience. Most recently, I was a guest lecturer at a university in Minneapolis, Minnesota. The night before the lecture, I was taken to the site of George Floyd's murder. May I quickly offer how very surreal the experience was. It brought in bas relief for me the stark realities of the murderous atrocity that had taken place close to the very spot where I stood. The grief, the anger and even in a very strange way, the guilt I felt, while being there, were palpable. I felt intrusive to be standing there as a spectator, almost disturbing a sacred site. Additionally, I experienced guilt for living in such a way where I could almost, but not most assuredly, escape and distance myself from the gruesome fatality George Floyd suffered. The conflation of emotions worsened when I returned to the site the following day after my lecture.

My host and I met a woman who took it upon herself to be a kind of spokesperson, caretaker, even ombudsman for the memorial area. She told us that her major responsibility was to see to it that people never forgot what had happened here. She had retired and believed that God had commissioned her to serve every day in this capacity. She believed so strongly that this was her divine assignment and was compelled to speak especially to visitors about her role as the "rememberer." To this divinely assigned woman, the atrocity of George Floyd's murder simply could not be forced to a back seat of the American consciousness and indeed she was going to see to it that that did not happen. This woman unashamedly admitted that this was her calling. This was a significant part of her destiny, and she was committed, against any level of opposition, to stand her watch diurnally, to ensure that her commission was fulfilled. On that day, the noonday sun was blazing, and the humidity was palpable. Standing and listening to the testimony of this woman was physically and emotionally uncomfortable. And yet this woman was undeterred from fulfilling her mission to educate us visitors and to keep alive her arduous task of constantly memorializing George Floyd's murder. It was as if she wanted us to deeply experience the discomfort. She wanted us to be ill at ease with our standing on these hallowed grounds. She pushed us academics to see what she saw outside of some objective, varnished and intellectually absent perspective from the grave realities of the hallowed site. She also advised us to go down the street and around the corner to see the panoply of tombstones in a field, of Black and Brown men and women, each with a person's name, age, when they were killed by law enforcement and the city where it had taken place. Eight rows, some with 20 tombstones, filled the field. Again, I sensed my own intrusion into a sacred space with the attitude of grace that had been extended to me as an African American man who had not even come close to being a name on one of those tombstones.

Undoubtedly, some readers may query just what this experience has to do with educational leadership and why it should be included in a work on critical spirituality and leadership. Allow me then to reiterate that educational leadership hardly comfortably resides in a frictionless environment. As I stood in the field of painful memories and denied dreams, I was consumed by the thought of how and if this moment in time, this moment in progressive poignancy, the schools in Minneapolis had included this painful event in their curriculum. How were they allowing the students, the teachers and even the parents to process what had happened in this city? I wondered how and if school leaders had accepted the responsibility of being the "rememberers" for their educational sites and were they being stalwart in their commitment not to allow their school communities to forget; not to allow the collective conscience of their communities to disremember the grave significance of what had taken place in their city.

Additionally, I wondered how schools and school leaders, external to Minneapolis, held vigil enough to include these events in their curriculums and their leadership behaviors. Including these kinds of events into the very fabric of the school's curriculum causes the students to know several important things. First, they know that what goes on outside of the school can be accessed inside the schoolhouse with the anticipation of it being interrogated, discussed, and engaged in both an academic and affective way. In other words, the school does not voluntarily divorce itself from the lived realities of the students, teachers, and administrators inside its walls. Additionally, the school does not take a dispassionate stance regarding the events that have impacted the community but reports them and then requires the school community to reflect and feel the impact of these events personally. Second, it demonstrates that the act of educating is one that has relevance. It is one that understands the primacy of aligning what is going on in the classroom with what happens in the community. It erases the exogamous notion that education prepares one to escape from the circumstances of one's life but instead provides a way to deal, to deconstruct and then to dismantle the circumstances and to use academic tools to create new ones. Education, therefore, has a utility, a service, and a practicality that surpasses the learning of inane bits of information that are disjointed from the realities of students' lived experiences. However, this utility can only be fomented through a prophetic ambience.

Earlier in this text the whole notion of leaders practicing their craft from a prophetic motivation was mentioned illustrating one of the ways that leadership can be a very critically spiritual engagement. I would like to return to that thought of the prophetic alignment with leadership to broaden the notion of prophecy and its role in situating leaders in a critical spiritual leadership space. I feel compelled to do this because I strongly believe that critical educational leadership must have a very prophetic edge to it. It must speak pointed truth to the current contexts of the education enterprise and yet announce a time ahead that is ensconced in the hopes for a better future. James Darsey (1997), in his insightful work, *The Prophetic Tradition and Radical Rhetoric in America*, compels the reader to engage with the notion of radical. Darsey does a spectacular job in locating the work of prophecy in explaining national American epochs. He unashamedly argues that the authentic function of a genuine prophet is to serve as a critic of the current and prognosticate the future using the lens of righteousness and justice as its perspective. Darsey helps us to understand that the prophet, as radical, simply compels them to declare what is at the root or the very foundation of an entity. This means that the prophet has had to explore what amounts to the core and even the very motivation for the existence of what has been established over time. It is the prophet's responsibility to declare that core or motivation and to guide the explored entity to that foundation. This is what, in Darsey's mind, constitutes the radical nature of the prophet.

While I understand and for the most part agree with Darsey's position on radical, I am nonetheless compelled to push back and to offer that while the radical inclination is to unearth what has been established as foundational, it seems also obligatory that the radical prophet questions the morality of the foundation, questions the justice of the foundation, its intent and its supposition of who should be included with what residuals or results. To leave untouched the very predisposition of the foundation explains why, in the years following, the entity has been engulfed in propagating undemocratic, supremacist and inequitable policies and practices.

There is no doubt that when one grounds leadership in a critically spiritual context there is concomitantly a commitment, on the individual's part, to walk in a radical tradition. This can be a very dangerous professional position to adopt because the whole notion of radical critically questions everything. It dismantles and actively disrupts what has been deemed to be foundational. It manages to defame what has been characterized as being worthy of reification and quickly places the individual, who does so, in a space of opposition to almost all that has been recognized as essential to the very foundation of what it means to lead. Indeed, this is the epitome of sacrilege. The whole idea of denying what has been called sacred in schools means that the leader has offered an antithesis to what has been historically touted as the very foundation of education and its leadership. And that antithesis is so different that it questions almost everything that has established the institution in the first place. That is a very daunting task. However, that kind of critical questioning, that kind of critical interrogation is essential to getting at the root of education and to initiate the process of naming what has been wrong with the institution from its very beginning. This radical disposition is at the very root of the personality of the prophet and causes the prophet to be in a constant state of agitating. There is always, in the prophet's mind, room for change. There is always room for organizational metamorphosis. There is always an area that needs attention, that needs to be transformed, guided by a commitment to see the educational institution as one that practices equity and justice for everyone impacted by the enterprise. It is much what Wendell Phillips says about the work of the prophet. He writes, "If we now repudiate and denounce some of our institutions, it is because we have faithfully tried them and found them deaf to the claims of justice and humanity" (p. 77). Over the years, scholars and practitioners have tried and found the institution of education deaf to the claims of justice and humanity through the many, many practices that sort, label, permanently position, and caste students in specific social and academic spaces forever.

Before we leave this notion of the prophetic edge and critically spiritual educational leadership, it is essential for us to understand that critique without offering a suggested resolution reduces the words of the prophetic to empty rhetoric without substantive steps to rectify what has been named to be problematic. Once any part of the educational process is troubled, then the leader who is grounded in a prophetic perspective is compelled to offer what is not yet but is possible. Recently I have been devouring Keith Boykin's (2021) *Race Against Time: The Politics of a Darkening America*. I have been captivated by a phrase he used to describe former President, Bill Clinton. In his chapter on Bill Clinton's Calculated Triangulation, he describes the former president as being either comforting or troubling. I find that description so very appropriate when characterizing the work and demeanor of the prophetic educational leader. For those who recognize the validity of the prophetic critique, such behavior for them is comforting. For those who are opposed to the position the prophetic leader is taking, to them the leader's behavior is troubling. The result of this prophetic edge to leadership is the inability to please but the calling to implement what is just, what is right, what is equitable. This therefore leads to the very last element of a school leader's repertoire that I want to cover.

Much of this text has focused on a leader's need to engage with the external exigencies that impact what takes place inside schools. Unashamedly, I have positioned the school leader's work as one that must contend or even comply with the multiple external forces that are screaming for attention. They will not be placated through avoidance or from being paid lifeless platitudes. Indeed, if that is the careless response to their presence, they will simply augment their volume and let the school leader know, without ambiguity, that they will not be ignored. This is most definitely a fact in a school leader's life. What concomitantly cannot be ignored is the leader's internal environment. What cannot be bereft of attention is the leader's predispositions, grounding principles and values that establish the contours of their professional behaviors. So, it is this internal landscape that will capture our attention.

I vividly remember when I was teaching graduate students preparing for the principalship that I so often told them that I was not about simply to tell them what to do on Monday morning but rather to get them to grapple with why what they want to do on Monday morning is the right thing to do. For some of my students, this was a frustrating exercise as they desired the litany of mechanical things to do when becoming the principal without giving much thought to discovering if the list of technical to-dos was the right thing to do and for whom did this list include the right things to do. I was asking the students to explore their internal environment and to come to grips with what suppositions forged the list and how humane were the various elements on that list of things to do. Allow me to show how important that internal investigation is to the work of the educational leader.

Michael Eric Dyson (2021) wrote a profound statement in the introduction to his book *Entertaining Race: Performing Blackness in America*. It captivated my thinking and confirmed the thinking of Frank Wilderson's position in his book, *Afropessimism*. Dyson wrote:

> Black life takes shape in a white world where stereotypes empty Blackness of all meaning except what benefits the broader world. That means that Black folk only exist when they are forced to adopt a narrow philosophy of life that is part Descartes, part Nas: Ut praestare, ergo sum, I perform, therefore I am. (p. 4)

The whole idea of exploring our internal landscape begs the question, do we perform, and our performance defines our existence or do we exist and out of the abundance of our being, grounded in our personal ontology, our performance or our teleology has come. It is vitally important for a school leader, who is impacting the lives of countless numbers of people, to reflect on the essence of their performance, to see that they are not performing, having been drained of their very being, but rather their very being drives them to perform as radically, critically spiritual, prophetic educational leaders. Who they are is not defined by performance but, on the contrary, their performance is grounded in who they are.

Along with clearly recognizing the impact of the external environment on an educational leader's practice, must also be the contending with one's internal environment. There is an adage that I have spoken, and I believe applies to this surveillance of one's internal state and it is, out of the abundance of the heart, the mouth speaks. When I consider my own practice as a Pre-K-12 school administrator and my positions of leadership in higher education, I know that the condition of my heart or the climate of my core manifested itself in the words I spoke, the decisions I made and the practices I implemented. I am not suggesting that a leader's behavior is susceptible to mood swings or frivolous presumptions, whims, or thoughtless assessments. Rather, our work as educational leaders stems from a reconciliation among what our heart knows to be right, what the institution demands and the impact of our internal composition on those with whom we interface. An educational leader is not an isolate and while our core must be under constant surveillance, we nonetheless are accountable for how our thinking and practices impact others. Let me share an example that I will retrieve from the last position I held in higher education.

As a dean of a college, I was compelled to make multiple decisions each day. Unfortunately, some required very little thought while others demanded the wisdom of Solomon to discern. One of the critical areas of decision-making for a dean is the matter of faculty promotion and tenure. I recall, before becoming a dean, that one of my colleagues shared, with me that the most significant job of a dean was the hiring, retaining and ultimately the tenuring process of faculty. I, indeed, believed that was an important facet of the dean's work but perhaps not as crucial or as far-reaching as my colleague had advised. Over my years as dean, however, I came to discover the accuracy of my colleague's sage wisdom.

Several of the most stressful decisions I made were in promotion and tenure cases. As I reflect upon these cases I am drawn to parse the three driving forces that conflate when a leader makes a significant decision. I made a very difficult decision that placed my decision-making process under the scrutiny of not only the provost but general counsel and the president of the university. I broke the unspoken protocol by deciding against the recommendations of department colleagues to support these cases and provided, what I believed to be crucial evidence to support my decision not to. These decisions caused me to see the contention of three driving forces that I will call the core, the constitution, and the constituent.

The core impetus is defined by my personal belief system, my dispositions, the standards I have come to establish as my guideposts for drawing such conclusions. My core is built upon my personal and professional conscience. It is the grounding for my authenticity and the substratum of my genuine self. The core is the repository of my history. It includes the very essence of my soul. It stores the foundation for my will and my emotions and is enriched by my spiritual heritage. The core has been built upon my cultural artifices that have created my mental and emotional agreements and beliefs for my life's interactions. My core is the evidence for the existence of my ontology. My core is enlivened through my experiences as a Black man and measures almost any issue from the annals and chronicles of my Black life. And though my core demands constant vigilance and surveillance to ascertain just how true my behaviors are to it, for so many of my actions, I must admit that the core is the motivation for what I do.

It was during these trying cases that I was bombarded by the constitutional force. This is the influence engendered by institutional policies and practices that hold legal weight and accountability for a leader's actions. Interesting how the constitutional presence really does not concern itself with the leader's core. The motivation for the constitutional impetus simply is to avoid litigation. The constitutional bent feigns an objectivity that cannot possibly exist because it is the institution that this motivation is determined to protect. So often, there is an unresolvable struggle between the core and the constitution. The constitution brings to bear the dichotomies that exist between itself and the core. Many a decision to leave the institution has been generated because of this contentious dynamic between one's core and the organization's constitution. Though my core was exceptionally active throughout this process, it, nonetheless, was vital for me to ensure that all the I's were dotted and all the Ts were crossed and that I did not breach any part of the prescribed policies that governed promotion and tenure. The force of constitution pretends a blindness to matters of race, gender, and even positional standing within the institution. However, I perceived that as a Black man, making these decisions especially about white members of the faculty demanded my more detailed commitment to following the process without deviation.

Finally, the third force, I call the constituent force. There is some relationship between the core and the constituent because the constituent focus causes the leader to grapple with the human exigencies that result from a decision. I was not heartless nor emotionally barren when faced with making these decisions. I was impacted by the fact that the people's and indeed their families' livelihoods would be subjected to my decision. That weighed heavily on me and was not easily ignored, though the constitutional focus that wanted to be the leading motivation, did not allow for such empathetic leanings. Funny how even now, of all the decisions I had to make as a dean, I rely upon this one to elucidate the presence of these three very powerful influences when deciding. May I quickly add that these three don't take turns in demanding one's attention. Throughout the process, they conflate, collide, and collude in multiple ways and honestly leave you drained and wondering if it was worth it to take this position.

Announcing the conclusion of the matter is not as important as understanding the process that took place to bring the matter to a conclusion. Whatever victory means was very hollow when considering the hard-hitting fact that people's lives were deeply impacted by that decision and the process that followed. But that is a crucial fact of leadership. It involves making decisions that will compel the core, the constitution, and the constituent elements to go to war with one another and to know that the conclusion of the matter only brings a fleeting armistice among the constantly competing influences.

Throughout this book, I have worked to demonstrate the intricacies of educational leadership. While I have focused our attention mostly on leading educational spaces, I contend that the lessons articulated within these pages can be applied to anyone who holds a leadership assignment. Indeed, what is really the crux of this work is the essential recognition of both the external and internal contexts of a leader's life that contend for prominence and domination in the leader's mind. Additionally, I have made the case that well beyond the intellectual or the mental appurtenances that leaders must possess, there is the spiritual endowment each person can embrace that serves as a phenomenal influence on the leader's practice.

Leadership, especially in these troubled times of perpetual conflict, must stem from a critical position when executing its performance. There are innumerable societal ills that deeply impact what happens in schools. Those forces simply cannot be ignored but must be engaged as pivotal influences on the educational process. Not to openly deal with these challenges leaves the educative process bereft of relevance and fails to prepare our students to face and then to discover and create ways to attend and ultimately to ameliorate these societal issues. Educational leadership that does not shy away from these battles but sees them as potent sources for academic labor is what is essential in these times. To do less is a fraudulent imprimatur of what educational leadership is all about.

REFERENCES

Adiche, C. N. (2021). Now is the time to talk about what we are talking about. In J. Cobb & D. Remnick (Eds.), *The matter of black lives: Writing from the new yorker* (pp. 99–104). Harper Collins.

Bell, D. (2002). *Ethical ambition: Living a life of meaning and worth*. Bloomsbury.

Boggs, G. L. (2011). *The next American revolution*. University of California.

Boykin, K. (2021). *Race against time: The politics of a darkening America*. Bold Type.

Buber, M. (1970). *I and thou* (W. Kaufmann, Trans.). Touchstone.

Capper, C. A. (2019). *Organizational theory for equity and diversity: Leading integrated, socially just education*. Routledge.

Dantley, M. E. (2005). African American spirituality and Cornel West's notions of prophetic pragmatism: Restructuring educational leadership in American urban schools. *Educational Administration Quarterly, 41*(4), 651–674.

Darsey, J. (1997). *The prophetic tradition and radical rhetoric in America*. New York University.

Fluker, W. B. (1999). The politics of conversion and the civilization of Friday. In Q. H. Dixie & C. West (Eds.), *The courage to hope: From black suffering to human redemption* (pp. 103–120). Beacon.

Foster, W. (1986). *Paradigms and promises: New approaches to educational administration*. Prometheus.

Freire, P. (1970). *Pedagogy of the oppressed*. Continuum.

Givens, J. R. (2021). *Fugitive pedagogy: Carter G. Woodson and the art of black teaching*. Harvard.

Grant, A. (2021). *Think again: The power of knowing what you don't know.* Penguin Random House.

Gutek, G. L. (1988). *Education and schooling in America.* Prentice Hall.

Harrison, G. P. (2013). *Think: Why you should question everything.* Prometheus.

Heifetz, R. A. (1999). *Leadership without easy answers.* Harvard.

Hill-Collins, P. H. (2013). *On intellectual activism.* Temple University.

Marable, M. (1998). *Black leadership.* Columbia University.

Meacham, J. (2020). *His truth is marching on: John Lewis and the power of hope.* Random House.

Obama, B. (2020). *A promised land.* Crown.

Smith, M. D. (2020). *Stakes is high: Life after the American dream.* Bold Type.

Thurman, H. (1958). *Meditations of the heart.* Beacon.

Thurman, H. (1976). *Jesus and the disinherited.* Beacon.

Walters, R. W., & Smith, R. C. (1999). *African American leadership.* State University of New York.

Watkins, W. H. (2001). *The white architects of black education: Ideology and power in America, 1865–1954.* Teachers College.

West, C. (1982). *Prophesy deliverance: An Afro-American revolutionary Chrstianity.* Westminster.

West, C. (1988). *Prophetic fragments.* Eerdmans.

White, J. L. & Cones, J. H. III. (1999). *Black man emerging: Facing the past and seizing a future in America.* Routledge.

Wilderson, F. B. (2020). *Afropessimism.* Liveright.

Wilkerson, I. (2020). *Caste: The origins of our discontents.* Random House.

Zamalin, A. (2019). *Black utopia: The history of an idea from black nationalism to Afrofuturism.* Columbia University.

INDEX

A

accountability 25
acrid critique 24
actualization, of ontology 46
African American spirituality
    academic mediocracy toward academic achievement 41
    assertion of, humanness 37, 38
    axiological capability 40
    of Black leaders 34
    Black Lives Matter Movement 39
    for black parents 31
    Black Power Movement 39
    buttressed by, leadership in 35
    Civil Rights Movement 35, 39
    critical self-reflection 33
    critical theoretical language 33
    dichotomy 32
    doctoral program 32
    elementary schools 30
    to embrace, ontology 36
    emergence of agency 40, 41
    explicity to 30
    exploration of 35
    hard-hitting truths 29
    hegemonic notions 33
    historic landmark in 31
    middle arbitrators with 32
    national prominence 42
    notion of Black Utopia 38
    notion of I/Thou 47, 48
    ontological sovereignty 42
    public-school administrator 29
    superintendent 31, 32
    supremacist machinations 40
    tenets of Frankfurt School 34
    transferred to magnet school 30, 31
    turbulent waters of ontology for 35
agency 40–43
aggrandizement 2
aggressive pessimism 27, 28
anchoring
    black leaders 23
    leader's behavior of 22

INDEX

oppositional thinking of 22
antediluvian leadership
  beyond our extant knowledge 77
  courage 82
  critical spirituality 80, 81
  divergently to 77
  epistemological certainty to 77
anti-Black racism 23, 26
antiphonal response 21
assimilationist 24
axiology, definitions of 45

B

Bell, D. 10, 11
black spirituality 2
Boggs, G. L. 27
Boykin, K. 90
Buber, M. 47, 48

C

calling
  aggressive in 21
  antiphonal response 21
  creation of vision 21
  existential nature of 22
  inherent in 22
  of prominence 24
  spiritual phenomenon 21
Capper, C. 7
casteism 46
colorblindness 8
compunction 5
Cones, J. H. III 20
constituent force 93
contour relationships 22
creativity
  educational leader 67
  encourages leader to 66
  to momentarily suspend rules and regulations 66

transformed future for 67
vision transformation 66
critical contemplation 6
critical self-reflection 21, 27
  analysis of 60, 61
  awareness process 63
  contextual influences with 60
  education's landscape 54
  endeavor of 53
  environment influences 52
  inquiries of 58
  leadership 54, 55
  process of 51
  result of 64
  scared self 59
  significant circumstances and substantive influences 60
  skepticism for 61
  time for 58
  ventures on 60
  witness 52, 53
critical spirituality
  performance creativity 65
  speaking/writing revelations 66
  to transform existing realities 66
critical theoretical lens 7

D

Darsey, J. 67, 89
dehumanization 40
democracy 79
disenfranchisement 3, 21
Dyson, M. E. 91

E

educational leadership
  abandon leadership to 1
  antithetical to 18
  capacity to engage 15
  characteristics of 16, 17

cognizant of contexts 5
community issues 4
compilation of 5
complex interplay of elements 5
complexities inherent in 17
   to define 1
demonstrations of democracy 16
   exploration of 16
financial aggrandizement of 19
in frictionless evironment 10
graduate courses in 6
hegemonic definitions of 17
   to implement 1
litany of 16
monumental benefits in 18
   to motivate 16
motivation and inspiration of
   individuals 11
poignant discussion on 18
quadrants and measurable behaviors 15
radical approach 7
risk of, potential efficacy of priming 1
scaffolding of 19
scholarly contributions to 6
sexualization of 17
social and political landscape 4
speaking truth and anger
   contextualizes 10
spiritual epicenter 1
spiritual reality of 20
victimization of 19
ways of thinking 1
enculturation 77–79
environmental scan 20
ethical decision-making 45

F

faithful ideation 46, 47
federal leadership 2
Floyd, G. 87
Fluker, W. 62
Freire, P. 55, 74, 75

frustration, anxiety and exceptional
   levels of 22
future orientation 25, 26

G

Giroux, H. 32, 33
Givens, J. 71
Glaude, E. 54, 57, 58
Grant, A. 56
Gutek, G 43–45

H

Harrison, G. P. 61
Heifetz, R. 19
humanitarian travesty 81
humanity 47
human oppression 21
humbling concession 55

I

imagination 25
individual's personality 10
inherent 22
   in orientation 24
intentional leadership 27
internal necessity 22

J

Jewish children 73

L

leadership, in education
   administration scholars 70
   attendance in 72

compulsory to attend school 72
contemplation on 73
hegemonic view of 71
intellectual process 76
land ownership 76
mechanism for enculturation 77
schools were deemed to 70
stage opportunity 73
teachable moments 74
teacher 74
leading
   attention on 94
   in broader context 22
   educational institutions 18, 65
   educational sites 1
   embroidered tapestry of 69
   impetus for 22
   Lewis, C. J., march on Bloody Sunday 17
   matter of contending with contexts 85
   motivation 94
   school/educational sites 71
   technical demands of 11
Lewis, C. J. 17, 18, 20

M

Marable, M. 26
marginalization 6, 40
masculinity 27
McLaren, P. 32, 33
medical professionals 4
microaggressions 40
monogamous fellowship 27
moral behavior 44
moral fiber 3

N

narcissistic pathology 3
national leadership
   disguise of 4
   paucity of 3

O

ontological sovereignty 42
oppression 3

P

patriotism 77
performative creativity 65
perpetuated racism 25
potential bifurcation 9
preservation 77
proclamation 26
project 41
Prophesy Deliverance 33
prophetic assessment 24
prophetic labor 25

R

racist macroaggressions 23
racist microaggressions 23

S

self-determination 45
self-inflicted castigation 21
self-integration 45
self-realization 45
Smith, M. D. 18
social interactions 77
spiritual aggrandizement 65
spiritual epicenter 1
spirituality
   of African American 5, 7, 20
   concept of communities of hope 19
   exogamous nature of 20
   forbidden realm of 2
   foundation in 2
   oxymoronic nature of 20
   role of 2

scholars of 12, 13
significance of 20
stage for 19
tenets of 7
spiritual motif 2
Student Nonviolent Coordinating Committee (SNCC), 17

T

teleology 42
Thurman, H. 10

W

Watkins, W. 75, 76
West, C. 19, 20, 25, 33
White, J. 20
Wilderson, F. 38, 39, 91
Wilkerson, I. 45, 46, 57, 58, 62

Z

Zamalin, A. 39, 40

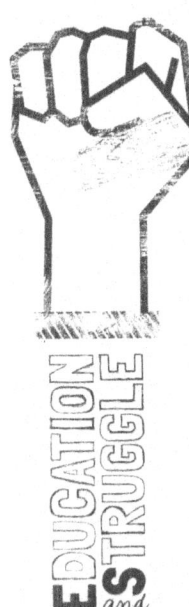

Narrative, Dialogue, and the Political Production of Meaning

Michael A. Peters
Peter McLaren
Series Editors

To submit a manuscript or proposal for editorial consideration, please contact:

Dr. Peter McLaren
Chapman University
College of Educational Studies
Reeves Hall 205
Orange, CA 92866

Dr. Michael A. Peters
University of Waikato
P.O. Box 3105
Faculty of Education
Hamilton 3240
New Zealand

WE ARE THE STORIES WE TELL. The book series Education and Struggle focuses on conflict as a discursive process where people struggle for legitimacy and the narrative process becomes a political struggle for meaning. But this series will also include the voices of authors and activists who are involved in conflicts over material necessities in their communities, schools, places of worship, and public squares as part of an ongoing search for dignity, self-determination, and autonomy. This series focuses on conflict and struggle within the realm of educational politics based around a series of interrelated themes: indigenous struggles; Western-Islamic conflicts; globalization and the clash of worldviews; neoliberalism as the war within; colonization and neocolonization; the coloniality of power and decolonial pedagogy; war and conflict; and the struggle for liberation. It publishes narrative accounts of specific struggles as well as theorizing "conflict narratives" and the political production of meaning in educational studies. During this time of global conflict and the crisis of capitalism, Education and Struggle promises to be on the cutting edge of social, cultural, educational, and political transformation.

Central to the series is the idea that language is a process of social, cultural, and class conflict. The aim is to focus on key semiotic, literary, and political concepts as a basis for a philosophy of language and culture where the underlying materialist philosophy of language and culture serves as the basis for the larger project that we might call dialogism (after Bakhtin's usage). As the late V. N. Volosinov suggests "Without signs there is no ideology," "Everything ideological possesses semiotic value," and "individual consciousness is a socio-ideological fact." It is a small step to claim, therefore, "consciousness itself can arise and become a viable fact only in the material embodiment of signs." This series is a vehicle for materialist semiotics in the narrative and dialogue of education and struggle.

To order other books in this series, please contact our Customer Service Department:

    peterlang@presswarehouse.com (within the U.S.)
    orders@peterlang.com (outside the U.S.)

Or browse online by series:

    www.peterlang.com

www.ingramcontent.com/pod-product-compliance
Lightning Source LLC
Chambersburg PA
CBHW061720300426
44115CB00014B/2765